David Gray

A Biography

Michael Heatley

David Gray

A Biography

Michael Heatley

OMNIBUS PRESS

London/New York/Paris/Sydney/Copenhagen/Madrid/Tokyo

Exclusive Distributors
Music Sales Limited,
8/9 Frith Street,
London W1D 3JB, UK.

Music Sales Corporation,
257 Park Avenue South,
New York, NY 10010, USA.

Macmillan Distribution Services,
53 Park West Drive,
Derrimut, Vic 3030,
Australia.

To the Music Trade only:
Music Sales Limited,
8/9 Frith Street,
London W1D 3JB, UK.

Every effort has been made to trace the copyright holders of the photographs in this book but one or
two were unreachable. We would be grateful if the photographers concerned would contact us.

Typeset by Phoenix Photosetting, Chatham, Kent
Printed in Great Britain by Creative Print & Design, Wales

A catalogue record for this book is available from the British Library.

Visit Omnibus Press on the web at www.omnibuspress.com

Contents

Prologue

Everyone who's interested enough to pick up this book – regardless of whether or not you've yet bought it – will have their own recollection of where and when they first heard David Gray.

My own epiphany came while browsing in a record shop in Winchester. The voice seemed somehow familiar. Bob Dylan, wasn't it? But no. The Zim would never have had any truck with such a hi-tech backing. What the? Who the? Paul Brady, maybe? Not American, certainly, but not quite Irish. Who the? What the? All right, I give in. . .

The man behind the counter thrust the jewel case towards me. David Gray. 'White Ladder'. He was used to the uncomprehending look, he'd been through this loop many times before. Indeed, putting this on the shop stereo system was a way of livening up his day – not to mention boosting sales when business failed to boom.

(Since then, I've seen John Cusack on *High Fidelity* use the same tactic with the Beta Band in his Championship Vinyl shop. Believe me, it was art imitating life!)

Back in Winchester, I was hooked. And the fact that the guy had released another three albums without me hearing about them let alone hearing them only added to the allure. When my friendly record retailer advised me these were otherwise unavailable, my detective instincts clicked in. What happened next began the trail that leads to this book you hold.

1

Gray has resolutely refused to discuss where his songs "come from" or his "ultimate goals" as a performer. When pushed, he will reveal that "Most of my songs are lit by the wonder of being alive. Even if that means feeling blue. Ultimately you do, as a singer, want to transport people, make that connection." He made it with me that day, and an article by Pat Kane reproduced in Chapter 11 explains most lucidly how he made it with millions more.

David Gray may not inspire as many books to be written about him as Bob Dylan. As far as I'm aware this is the first of them. Whatever he does, he has already contributed to the rich tapestry we know as popular music, and for helping ensure the singer–songwriter enjoys a reasonably high profile during the first years of the current millennium, I thank him.

INTRODUCTION

The Point of No Return

When David Gray released his *White Ladder* album on his own label at the start of 1999, he did so only in Ireland. Having gone through two record labels during the course of his three previous recording ventures, he had no illusions about dominating the world of pop – at least not in the foreseeable future. Ireland, though, was the one place that had taken to his raw, confessional style without reservations, and it seemed as good a place as any to start re-climbing the musical Matterhorn down which he'd inexorably been slipping.

But miracles do happen. By the end of the year he was a fully-fledged star on the other side of the water from his place of birth. U2's Bono, among others, was endorsing his music – a recommendation that 8,500 fans were happy to follow by buying every seat in Dublin's Point Depot venue. That December 1999 gig will forever remain a watershed in his career.

"It was one long succession of pleasing synergies – people being in the right place at the right time, the band coming together, things like that," he'd tell *Hot Press* music paper a few months later. "But the Point gig was just a monumental night – the culmination of years of passionate support from the fans, and of blood, sweat and tears on our behalf."

He'd started again at the bottom after an Irish DJ Donal Dineen had picked up on 'Shine', his earliest professional recording, and made it the theme tune to his show, RTE's *No Disco*. After being over-whelmed with requests for more, he invited David to play in Whelan's of Wexford Street in Dublin. Gray admits he felt the emotionally charged atmosphere raise the hairs on the back of his neck. "There were a few moments when the crowd went completely ballistic and it was like, 'Wow! This is *serious*.' It was truly awe-inspiring! The audience bring to it what they will; that night, they were fantastic and all I had to do was not blow it."

He could do no wrong on that occasion, but the challenges rocket-propelled stardom threw up would prove more difficult for an inti-mate singer-songwriter type to overcome. "I'm working on my stage projection," he'd admit, while allowing that both he and his fans would have to adapt. "The situation has changed. It's moved on a few paces, so we're just trying to keep things interesting. You can't please all the people all the time. We wanted to have a big party and get the most amount of people as we could at it."

Yes, the future would be different, but Dublin would remain for-ever in his heart. So much so that he'd return to play a free Millennium gig on December 31, 1999 for those who couldn't get Point tickets. Roll on another 12 months and, far from being the up-and-coming songwriter of early 1999, he was well known world-wide, had a Top 10 single in his home country and was strongly tipped to conquer the States. The Point had given him that first glimpse of what the future could be. "There are certain times when you see the future and you step into bigger shoes. You have to cast the skin of insecurity aside. It was like, come on, let's go – why not us instead of some other band?"

The Irish audience offered him the stepping stone he needed. "It's been such a long-running story. I've been adopted by them because I've toured so extensively, far beyond what you're expected to do, because I really wanted to. I didn't want to go back to England, where I was being ignored."

A gig in Galway in the middle of the year had attracted four and a half thousand people, giving him the platform to attempt the big-city gig at a venue only U2 and Boyzone could be guaranteed to fill. But like the rest of the David Gray story, it took a lot of people by surprise, himself included. "But it's like, why not? If you make something of spirit, it just goes out into the world and starts creating ripples. I just didn't realise the scale it was going to get to. It's been fantastic. And it's just getting started. . . there are more chapters to be written, I think."

All told, it was an unforgettable night to crown an incredible year. "Not so much a gig as a celebration. A moment when it all made sense, a stepping into bigger shoes, a taste of things to come."

Twenty months after the Point and a further none since its release, *White Ladder* had created history by reaching the top of the UK album chart – its passage there the longest since Tyrannosaurus Rex's *My People Were Fair And Had Sky In Their Hair. . .'*. That album had taken four years to reach Number 1, propelled there after Marc Bolan fans impatient for new product discovered an album that had reached no higher than Number 15 in its 1968 heyday but when linked with its even less successful follow-up, *Prophets Seers And Sages, The Angels Of The Ages*, had been reissued by a former record company to lucrative effect. With sales totalling 1,556,000 at the point it hit the top, *White Ladder* had achieved its success by appealing to those who didn't consider themselves record-buyers. It had become as much an album to be seen with as Fleetwood Mac's *Rumours* a quarter-century or so earlier. The difference was it had been created not in a series of glossy studios but on a shoestring budget in a terraced North London house.

But as *Rumours* listeners had taken the tales of relationships between Mac band members and applied them to their own lives, so the everyday tales on *White Ladder* spoke to listeners. *The Observer's* Pat Kane – himself a former pop star with Hue and Cry – termed the album "table-top therapy amid the Chardonnay, soggy joints and domestic bills".

Yet while groups like Fleetwood Mac could re-invent themselves over the years, the shelf life of the singer-songwriter tended to be a shorter one. Cat Stevens in the Seventies and Tanita Tikaram were just two examples of the genre who'd commanded Top Three chart positions and produced multi-million-selling albums, only to find themselves plummeting into obscurity as their audience grew up and moved on. That was the challenge facing David Gray – but as we shall see, he already had a couple of re-inventions under his belt before he found the winning formula.

Up to the Point, his instincts had served him well. . .

CHAPTER 1

Upbringing

David Gray was born in the south Manchester suburb of Sale in 1968 (many biographies have erroneously stated 1970, but an early Hut biography confirms the date) to a well-to-do family. He was one of three children, the other two girls, who lived in what he'd later call "a big fuck off house". Not the kind of background for a rebellious rock star, but the keynote of his upbringing was essentially middle class.

His grandfather owned a chain of bakery shops, and David's own father Peter worked with him in the family firm. It seems the intention was for the younger man to take over in time, but when David was eight what he's since fascinatingly termed "poisonous inter-family madness" caused a change of lifestyle. The decision was taken to move the family lock, stock and barrel to the remote Welsh county of Pembrokeshire.

Far from being upset at exchanging big-city bustle for rural tranquillity, the boy seemed to take to it. Indeed, that Welsh upbringing has been a big influence. "I'd be lying if I said I was Celtic, but it definitely was a formative thing for my psyche," he'd say in 1996. "It made a huge impression on me moving to Wales as a child, it formed me in so many ways. I felt immediately at home there, by the sea and in the woods."

In 2001, he recalled his childhood in more detail for *Rolling Stone* magazine. "We had this tiny little cottage with this shanty bit on the side that was the kitchen. I remember walking out the back when we first got there and climbing through the fence, and there was a hill going up, and then just woods, and you know how things seem a lot bigger when you're small? Well, I thought, 'Fucking hell, this is amazing. It's a forest. Action Man is going to have a brilliant time!' "

Something had certainly made a deep and abiding connection, and it wasn't long before he'd concluded that life in west Wales "was a million times better than living in the city. My imagination could run wild. I don't remember missing any of my friends at all, or missing anything."

The harbour village of Solva which he now called home was and is very small. Very little happened in winter, but it would become very popular in the summer with tourists stopping on their way to nearby St David's and its cathedral. His father had bought a local gift shop to cater for just that passing trade and David would help out from time to time when old enough to do so. Other part-time pocket-money jobs included washing dishes in a seafood restaurant and waiting on tables in a local bistro.

As with most children, his parents' record collection would strike an early chord. The Gray family favourites included "Singer-songwriters like Elton John, Cat Stevens, Carole King, that kind of thing. My mum used to listen to classical music. Dad listened to Frank Sinatra, The Beatles. . . So, I remember hearing that as I grew up. Then, I started listening to whatever was happening in 1979 and '80. I suppose that's when I started to be interested. I was about 10 or 11 . . . bands like the Specials. . . that kind of ska stuff."

He bought his first record in 1979 – the bombastic, chart-topping 'I Don't Like Mondays' by Bob Geldof's Boomtown Rats. "I just like it. Ridiculous song, really, but there you go" – while the band he was at first most into was Madness, whom he first saw on television's *Top Of The Pops* and whose *One Step Beyond* album was the first 'long-player' to enter his collection. "They were going absolutely mental, seven of them squashed on a tiny little stage, and every bastard in the house was dancing," Gray says of his heroes. "I learned all the dance moves."

All this was necessarily imbibed second-hand. Modern culture came to Solva courtesy of the cathode-ray tube, while trendy chain-stores and music venues were another world. "The danger of living in the middle of nowhere." he'd later reflect, "is that there's no cool people to judge your fantasy of what's cool, and there's also no shops to get the cool gear, so you're, like, tailoring your own two-tone gear with potato sacks – it's not easy."

Occasionally the locals would give him a good kicking for his trouble, one affronted Welshman pouring a pint over his head. More happily, he would display his artistic tendencies by drawing groups of Crombie-overcoated Madness-type figures while in school as well as liberally graffiti-ing the area with the 'M' logo. "I'm better at nutty dancing than they were!," he's since remarked, terming them "the first pop thing I became part of."

But Suggs's big-city boys eventually lost their appeal and David returned to his parents' record collection for more lasting inspiration. He can vividly recall one day "around 1980" being "transfixed" by the sound of Bob Dylan, "his acoustic recordings, in particular". It certainly wasn't his first exposure to the revered Sixties singer-songwriter. "My Dad had a Bob Dylan greatest hits album on in the car as we drove through France when we were kids" – but it was a telling one. "Since then," he admits, "I've heard just about all his albums. My favourite is 'Blonde On Blonde'. It's not such an easy album to listen to, there's a really harsh harmonica sound on it, it can blow your eardrums at times. 'Visions Of Joanna' and 'Sad Eyed Lady Of The Lowlands' are fantastic. *Blood On The Tracks* is another favourite of mine. Then there's *Oh Mercy* from his recent past, and the beginning of *Infidels* from the Eighties. He has consistently done it over the decades."

His other major songwriting hero was and remains Van Morrison. But in this case, he narrows his epiphany down to one album in particular – one which, ironically, came out in the year of his birth. "If there's a record which has profoundly affected me over a long period of time, it would be *Astral Weeks*. Once you've immersed yourself in that record and it's blown you away, you're never able to look at music in the same way again. It's not a record you go back to and say 'This is crap, I used to like this record', it's an acquired taste.

"The first time I heard it, I didn't get it, and somewhere along the line the penny dropped. I went through my 'Into The Mystic' phase and *Astral Weeks* just opened up for me. I can think of no greater moment of inspiration in popular music history. It's got the daftest ideas, like an out of time drummer, it's all in the charm of it. From start to finish, there's no other record like it."

While musical lessons were being learned, there was still the little matter of school and qualifications to attend to. The academic side of things came quite easily to David, though he admits to losing interest in formal learning at about 14. He was a bit of an all-rounder, being sporty enough to play football for the school team*. He's since described his school, the 350-pupil Ysgol Dewi Sant comprehensive, as pretty gentle, "with none of that terror of 1,500 mad teenagers waiting to battle you every time you leave the school gates."

A decidely offbeat sense of humour was beginning to come to the fore, too. David became a fan of Peter Cook and Dudley Moore after finding one of their expletive-flecked albums recorded under their Derek and Clive personae in his father's record collection when about 13. He then graduated to Alexei Sayle, the bald and fearsomely bearded member of the Young Ones whose 'Ullo John Gotta New Motor?' charted in 1984. David invested in a live album and was particularly taken by a track called 'Mr Sweary' which he blames for his current "40 a day swearing habit."

Writing poems and painting were his favourite occupations while at school. An early Hut Records biography dates his first brush with the guitar as 1984, when he "began playing and writing songs", and he confirms he was a quick learner. "As soon as I learned a few chords on the guitar I wanted to write songs – so I started putting words to the music." His father had a guitar that was lying around the house "so I picked that up. He wrote a few chords down and that was the beginning, basically. It's quite an easy instrument to learn, and you get immediate results."

Next step was to form a band. "I'd always been into amateur dramatics and stuff, school plays and things like that, and I liked all that side of it – being on stage, showing off and being stupid wasn't a

---

* An avid Manchester United supporter, it remains a major interest.

problem. So having a guitar and doing that seemed like the next log-ical step."

He started his first group, The Prawns, with three school-friends while in his mid teens; he played lead guitar and even secured per-mission to practice in the school gym. But practice, it seemed, did not make perfect straight away. They had the audacity to perform at school discos but did not go down especially well with their peers. "We played our first gig and people tried to kill us, we were so bad.

"It was a dance: everybody wanted boogie-woogie and we came on and murdered a load of Jimi Hendrix tunes; it was *ridiculous*. But I thought it was a fantastic thing, being hated by all the squares. Wear stupid clothes, make-up or whatever took our fancy. That was when I thought, 'Oh I like this,'" David (who'd augmented his guitar with a borrowed Casio keyboard) cheerfully recalls. His template for the band was American 'psychobillies' The Cramps. "We didn't really do our own stuff, we just played everything we could learn on the gui-tar. The mind boggles."

Now re-named The Vacuums – "We moved away from seafood and into domestic appliances" – the band's repertoire owed something to David's father's record collection – most notably a version of 'Won't Get Fooled Again', from The Who's seminal 1971 recording *Who's Next*. This was considerably more ambitious than either 'Substitute' or 'My Generation', two punk favourites from The Who's repertoire, since the original was based around a synthesiser part that ran throughout the song. David, who had no way of getting hold of a sequencer (and probably didn't know what one was, anyway), played the whole thing in real time on his Casio.

Little wonder their stage act was chaotic. "We were totally con-fused; we looked like total lunatics fucking about." One particular early gig, a beach party that happened every year, sticks in his mem-ory. "It was so exciting, like Woodstock to us, but it was really about 15 people in the pissing rain in Wales, with a generator that was louder than the band," he says with a laugh.

Things didn't get better, largely due to the diversity of musical dif-ferences within the ranks. David was so into The Cure at this point that he knew the words to every album, and was understandably keen to get the collected works of Robert Smith into the repertoire if he could. And being the leader, he could. "The guitarist was into The Who, the drummer wanted to play Led Zeppelin and Jimi Hendrix and I wanted to do The Cure or The Cramps, so it was always a compromise!"

With mutiny on the horizon, The Vacuums ended up dividing up the set to reflect the band members' tastes – even if the result was somewhat hard on the ear. "It was awful but fantastic fun!" David recalls. "We all used to put make-up on. Once, we played at a regatta in a marquee and everyone thought we were a covers band. We started playing utter shit with one amp between us."

Having been quizzed about these early days so often, David has distanced himself from some of his early descriptions – perhaps fearing zealous fans might attempt to locate and, horror of horrors, circulate Vacuums bootleg tapes. "We weren't a punk band," he insists, putting that label down to "a badly written bio kind of thing. . . it was just a crap band. We just sounded dreadful. We were loud and rubbish and that was basically our style."

Whether being in a band, crap or otherwise, gave David the edge when it came to attracting the opposite sex has never been made clear. But he would later recall "snogging at teenage parties and drinking cider" at the age of 13 or 14. The soundtrack to these first fumbling romantic explorations was Soft Cell's 'Say Hello, Wave Goodbye' – a song he would see fit to revisit in future years.

The local barn dances, run by large, sweaty farmers who fancied themselves as DJs, were the hotbeds of social interaction around Solva way. David would later recall "huge cowsheds that smelt of shit, straw in the pint and records like that horrible 'Stars On 45' or 'Agadoo'. And they'd roast a pig." The most attractive feature of such occasions was the chance to grab a few illicit shots of alcohol – "they'd serve you vodka and orange, even though you were four or five years off being alcohol drinkers."

A schoolboy needs contemporary heroes and, with Suggs, Bedders and company now a fast-fading memory, Gray supplemented Messrs Dylan and Morrison with a younger, sprightlier figure – Steven Morrissey. "I was a big fan at the time, as most people were, though I don't think (The Smiths) have aged very well. Everyone used to say, 'God, it's so miserable, Morrissey's so miserable' and I would say, 'No, it's brilliant.' But (now) I listen back and I think, 'God, it's so miser-able.'" He pinpoints 'How Soon Is Now?' ("an absolutely fantastic song") and the ballad 'Back To The Old House' (the B-side to 1984's hit 'What Difference Does It Make?') as particular favourites. Indeed, so enthusiastic was he that he travelled all the way to Edinburgh in 1985 to see his hero on The Smiths' *Meat Is Murder* tour. "Morrissey was throwing plants around on the stage. I had a piece of weed that he had thrown into the audience, which I treasured for years — until I suddenly realised it was just a dried-out bit of weed."

Just as the foliage shrivelled, so Gray's respect for Morrissey waned when he felt he was losing touch with reality. "When you hear something like 'Please, Please, Please, Let Me Get What I Want', you think, 'Wait a minute, you were a pop star, with loads of money, playing big shows. What are you talking about?'" If ever he made it, David Gray would remember to remain grateful for what he'd been given.

Next to impact on the live stage after The Smiths was Mike Scott and his band The Waterboys. David saw them in Manchester when they toured 1985's *This Is The Sea* and he recalls them being "a heavy-weight band then. They played for about two-and-a-half-hours, then started doing covers and jamming. I'd never seen that before. I'd seen The Smiths and it was great, but there was no passion about them. The Waterboys just kept on playing: it was fuckin' fantastic. I carried that gig with me for years. They were unlike anything else around at the time. They had the snare sound from hell, but it still stands up." This was, he concluded, "the most important gig I'd been to up to that point."

There's an interesting comparison to be made, in retrospect, between David Gray and Mike Scott. Both are individuals who have enjoyed a growing affinity with the Irish audience and derived inspi-ration from Celtic culture (Scott was born and grew up in Scotland). Both would pay overt homage to Van Morrison, and both would win Ivor Novello songwriting awards for songs that were only hits the second time around. Scott's was for 'The Whole Of The Moon', a 1985 release that finally made the Top Three in 1991.

Back in the late Eighties, David had left school with 'A' Levels in English Literature and Art – his key to art college, the breeding ground for so many great musicians before him. But first, come 1986, he had to take a year's foundation course at Carmarthen, commuting there from home. Next stop was the Liverpool College of Art (whose most famous ex-student to date was John Lennon), where he was sufficiently adept at painting to make £2,000 in a single summer through sale of work – a tidy sum which certainly helped supplement his grant.

His parents were very encouraging of their student son, little realising his cunning strategy. "I've always been very into doing my own thing and they never said 'you're not going to do this'. They were delighted I wanted to do things (because) I cocked up all my exams at school. I got bored with things because I knew what I wanted to do. So I worked out the path of least resistance – Art School! Brilliant! A few dodgy paintings and I'll be there: form a band and stone me! It all sort of worked."

Though he knew it was music he was going to pursue with greatest vigour, art has remained an abiding passion – the more so as pressures have grown. "I still love painting," he insists today. "Painting's a more solitary experience, and brilliant for it as well, but music opens doors to other people and that's what gives it the edge for me." His parents would nevertheless be delighted with their son's success. "My dad has been pretty intense about it. He's dead proud and he goes on about it and sometimes I'm like 'shut up, dad!' because he's telling everyone what's happening. But parents, they're embarrassing aren't they?"

Living in a converted Merseyside police station, David formed a series of college bands from 1988 onwards, the most notable being Waiting For Deffo. Liverpudlians might begin to get the joke, Deffo being the Scouse abbreviation for Definitely, but Gray is happy to explain for others. It all started one winter, he revealed, when building workers accidentally cut through their gas main, leaving the household bereft of heat and cooking facilities. Naturally he and his student pals were immediately on the phone to the gas board's emergency hotline. "I'd ring up and say, 'Look, when are you going to get the gas back on? We haven't any heat!' And they'd go, 'Oh, we'll be round there this afternoon, mate – Deffo'."

Once his blue fingers had thawed Gray, plus drummer 'Scottish

Bob' and a guitarist and bass player whose names have been lost in the mists of time, doggedly plied their musical trade round Liverpool's myriad rock venues. He'd just finished his degree when they amassed enough money to record a demo tape – a venture David would later describe to VH1 as "the turning point. We went in the studio and we only had enough money to pay for (a certain) amount of time. And we just ran out: we were still playing when the door opened and that was it. Right, it's all over. That was the demo, it was just ridiculous. We had this sax player playing on some of it, (but) there were no over-dubs, we couldn't do anything twice. We just played as quickly as possible."

They sent the resulting tape, with all its flaws, off to the *Manchester Evening News*, as well as sundry other regional rock critics, and received a surprisingly positive response. A couple of copies somehow reached the hands of record company A&R men (the talent scouts of the industry), one of whom – Rob Holden, then senior A&R with Polydor – would in time become David's manager. At the time, he had just had a motorbike accident and was in hospital. . . according to his future charge "out of his mind on some weird drug concoction. Someone handed him this tape and that was it – he heard something he liked. That was the start of the real thing. He went to his contacts and eventually ended up with a record deal, though not a particularly big one."

Even so, it was the culmination of a dream – and crucial enough for the eminently decent Gray to sack his fellow band members. Or did he simply walk out? Either way, it was clear that Holden had homed in on him as the creative hub of Waiting For Deffo. And the others would just have to wait their turn. "I split the band up," Gray admits with no little shame. "It was a bummer. I told them I was going to London to do a demo. I think I'm going to go with this manager guy. I did feel bad. But with the benefit of hindsight. . . well, the fucking guitarist was 39!"

Holden, who, according to Gray, "hobbled up to Liverpool on his crutches to see us", was impressed by David's impassioned vocal delivery but couldn't tell from the tape whether the singer was 16 or 60. Curiosity clearly got the better of him. "Then after that," he adds, "everybody disagreed with me about David's abilities for about eight years." Undeterred, and certain his charge was stardom-bound, Rob Holden quit the security of his Polydor post to go solo.

He had other irons in the fire, most notably brothers Paul and Phil Hartnoll who were making waves on the street-level dance-music scene. Convincing them to change their handle from DS Building Contractors to the infinitely more snappy Orbital, he'd see them mint a rave anthem in 'Chime' which started life as a 1,000-only pressing by indie label Oh-Zone and ended up on *Top Of The Pops* and in the Top 20.

On the face of it, Holden's charges had little if anything in common. But Phil Hartnoll's wife had a sister, Olivia, who'd figure large in David Gray's life further down the line, while Paul would use his remixing skills to turn one of David's songs into dancefloor dynamite. Not long afterwards would come the singles success that would set his slow-burning career alight. But 'Babylon' was still a long, long way away. . .

CHAPTER 2

Climbing The Ladder

With Rob Holden's guiding hand at his shoulder, David signed with Hut Records, a leading independent label. The association did him no harm at all on the credibility scale, Hut already having the likes of Smashing Pumpkins and The Verve on its books. Was David Gray getting trendy? Deffo, mate, deffo. . .

His first national tour came as support to labelmates The Auteurs, an ever so slightly pretentious but nevertheless critically acclaimed outfit led by one Luke Haines, a self-confessed "arty wanker". David has distinct memories of the jaunt round the UK and a few cross-Channel dates in France. He would follow the tour bus in his car, with his guitars on the back seat and a friend in the front "so I didn't go crazy with loneliness." The soundtrack for the jaunt was provided by Chrissie Hynde, a cassette copy of The Pretenders' *Singles* collection having been purchased at a French service station once they'd exhausted the contents of the glove compartment.

His relationship with Haines – a man memorably described by Hut boss Dave Boyd as "Ray Davies on Prozac" – was cordial enough, though his own nickname for him was Dracula due to his nocturnal habits. "He'd never come out of his room apart from at nights." When not on the move, David mixed happily with the other Auteurs

– cellist Dave Banbury, bassist Alice Readman and drummer Glenn Collins – and when they finally reached the Cote d'Azur the stage was set for all-night post-gig parties, "drinking beer and making fires." Another touring ritual was games of Scrabble, at which wordsmith Gray more than held his own until tragedy struck. "My mate jumped into a swimming pool with Haines' Scrabble set, to exclamations of fear from everyone (shouts) – That's Luke's set!"

Interestingly, David would follow in the footsteps of Seventies punk turned radio presenter Tom Robinson in ruffling the feathers of chief Kink Ray Davies when, in 1992, he received a short-notice phone call to support the noted Sixties hitmakers at no less a venue than the 4,000-capacity Royal Albert Hall in central London. For simplicity's sake, the brief was to play solo. "My agent had said we've got this guy, no problem with any technical shit, it's just a man and his guitar." (A configuration Davies himself would adopt while moonlighting as a rock'n'roll raconteur later in the decade.) So far so good – but when that man and his aforementioned instrument mounted the RAH stage, the venue's enormity must have got the better of him. "I said, 'Fuck 1969, this is 1992!' I thought I was going to stir it up. They just started heckling me. Who the fuck are you? Fuck off! Fuck off!"

Regardless of whether this little-known Dylan-esque performer had the right to label the assembled multitude Sixties throwbacks, it certainly polarised the audience – and pole-axed his manager, watching proudly from the Albert Hall wings. An interval showdown among the G&T set was inevitable. "Rob said, 'Why did you do that?' And I said 'I thought you'd be proud of me'. It was situationist." Certainly, Ray Davies (whom David then, as now, admires greatly) felt threatened enough to preface the headliners' set with a speech proclaiming that great music lasted forever. At least he didn't write a song about David, as he did Tom Robinson with 'Prince Of The Punks', though in view of Gray's subsequent and long-delayed fame, there's still time...

The following year would see him doing something similar to an audience that had gathered at another London venue, Dingwall's, to hear another venerated music-business veteran. The headliner this time was American folk singer Joan Baez, who'd signed with Virgin

Records and was on her way to her first critical acclaim in a decade and a half with the album *Play Me Backwards*.*

David had opened the show to typical disinterest from the fifty-something American's equally aged fans who had clearly heard of her ex-boyfriend Dylan but were less impressed by some bolshy young-ster who sounded a bit like him. "He was berating the audience for being boring and middle class," one unimpressed onlooker now recalls, "and I thought if you're that upset why don't you go and stack supermarket shelves or something?"

David's own gigs could be almost as entertaining – not least for what happened afterwards. One such at a Welsh rugby club close to home in 1992 saw him whip up some local support, only to find himself locked up in the cells for a night after he realised he'd left the keys to the band Transit van in the venue. He recruited an accomplice and sneaked back in through a rear window, but both disappeared rapidly when the burglar alarm went off. From their vantage point in the woods they surveyed the police-ridden scene, and eventually had to turn themselves over to the boys in blue as their brief spell 'inside' (the club, not jail) had failed to locate the missing keys.

"I walked in and there was a copper looking at a photo of one of my footprints," recalls David, who admits to being "completely off my head" at the time. In that case, maybe it was a good job he didn't end up behind the wheel! Instead, the hospitality of Fishguard Police Station was extended until he'd sobered up – and, for some while after that, he rejoiced in the local nickname of 'Footprint'.

Other gigs were almost deliberately unsuitable for a singer-songwriter and his acoustic guitar. Rob Holden, it seemed, had a plan. "He thought the worst crime we could commit was to be per-ceived as old-school folkies," Gray now says, "so I would only play gigs in the most inappropriate places. I was playing at raves. I remem-ber at one place there was free acid pinned to one of the doors, and I came on in the middle of this ridiculous hardcore groove to do a few numbers. It was like, 'Who? What?' Then people started to get into it

---

* She has since praised Gray as "the finest lyricist since Bob Dylan", though the occasion of this comment is uncertain.

somehow. Bizarrely, those gigs usually went all right." Maybe some of the dance grooves rubbed off in later years. . .

The route to a recording contract had taken him via a studio in north west London called the Power Plant. Run by Robin Millar, whose biggest claim to fame was discovering and producing early-'Eighties star Sade, it had a stable of young producers, one of whom was Dave Anderson. "Robin basically gave me my first job in the music business. A demo of David's from when he was still in his Liverpool band Waiting for Deffo, had been sent to Robin originally, who passed it on to me. I remember hearing it and thinking it was great. He wasn't signed at that point, so we started off doing a few demos and it took off from there."

Anderson's first task was to observe his future charge in concert on "a few supports and a few little things around London. He was quite an aggressive performer, David, but very emotional, very honest. All of it was great. The thing I thought was particularly attractive about doing the record was that this was very honest music – there was no artifice about it, it wasn't a pose. It was how he felt."

Having done a few demos in studio 'down time' at the Power Plant, the venue changed to Town House 3 studio in Shepherds Bush. "I don't know if we paid for it or if Rob Holden blagged it from someone," Dave Anderson admits, "but we had a day, maybe a couple of days and did three songs – one of which ended up on the record, which was the first version of 'Shine'. He got signed on the strength of that. And then fortunately they didn't wheel in someone else to produce the rest of the record, which often happens. We got the chance to basically do it ourselves – and we did."

Having proudly become a Hut recording artist, it was time for David to make his long-anticipated disc début. The choice of single was 'Birds Without Wings', another track cut in the early days which proved impossible to recapture with the same feel. When it was released in November 1992, it lacked any fanfare whatsoever; its fail-ure was therefore hardly surprising in a market crammed with sea-sonal novelties and soon to be dominated for an epic ten weeks by Whitney Houston's astonishingly popular disembowelling of Dolly Parton's 'I Will Always Love You'. 'Birds Without Wings' would never-theless become a long-time fan favourite and Q magazine's choice as standout track of the album to follow. At the time, though, Ms Houston hardly quaked in her designer footwear.

'Birds' began with a lazily strummed acoustic guitar and a distinctive delivery pitched somewhere between Irish folk-rock veteran Paul Brady and Lindisfarne's late, great Alan Hull. Somehow, David managed to swallow the first line's last word, "hap'n", while extending the fourth line's conclusion from package to "pack-ayge". The vibrato in his voice was something he'd later condemn as having been affected, but gave the impression of a singer rather older than his then relatively tender 24 years. Little wonder his manager-to-be had been confused. The song chugged along without an obvious chorus until the title phrase appeared halfway through as some kind of punctuation point – a regular Gray device, it would transpire.

The accusation of being somewhat downbeat was one he readily accepted. "There is a melancholic feel to a lot of my stuff. I suppose it's a natural thing. If you sit alone and quietly pluck your knackered old, wooden guitar, sad sounds usher forth. It is a sort of contemplative occupation."

The 'knackered old wooden instrument' David was using at this time was a 1961 Martin 000-18, the choice of virtuoso players like Eric Clapton and Steve Howe. It had a special significance in that he'd paid for it with the advance from a music publishing deal with Warner Chappell that had preceded his gaining a recording contract. "Acoustic guitars can be wild, boomy things when you get them in front of a mic," he said, "but this Martin seems to have calmed down with age. Must be the wood or something." Calming down was something the instrument's owner wasn't considering just yet.

Two songs nestled on the flip of what would, at the point in pop history when singles were flipped, have been termed an EP. 'L's Song' immediately lifted the sombre mood set by the A-side, boasting a slightly more complex and uptempo guitar figure. Addressed to a long-gone love, Gray pleaded for "one morsel/of your lovin' again". An overdubbed, mid-song solo acoustic guitar which recurred towards the end was the only indication that we were listening to anything other than one man and his guitar. On its reappearance in mid-2001, this was one of three early songs Gray would consider still stood up. As for L, her identity remains a mystery.

Arguably the most interesting of the three tracks, however, was 'The Light'. Counted in by Gray himself, it succeeded in introducing for the first time the keyboard and acoustic guitar mix that would later become his trademark – but, as yet, without the crucial looped percussion – and would later be re-recorded to become a highlight of his second LP, *Flesh*. The most uptempo track of all, it gave Gray the chance to sing more naturally and unselfconsciously. The repeated "come rollin'" at the end of the song inevitably evoked Dylan's 'Like A Rolling Stone', but the overall effect was impressive in predicting what was to come.

The release was celebrated by a four-week residency at London's Troubadour Club, the home of acoustic live performance. This sold out through what Hut's biography-writer quaintly termed "word of mouth advertising". "It was the agent's idea," Gray later recalled, "and I knew the people there so it was no problem to get the gigs. It was this idea they had to make it a really buzzing thing, but it didn't come off really. . ."

It followed on from an early singer-songwriter showcase opportunity at Ronnie Scott's Jazz Club in Soho, where he'd rubbed shoulders with any number of acoustic guitar-wielding folkies and not enjoyed the experience. The Troubadour residency did, however, attract the attention of Greater London Radio, the BBC local station since criminally transformed into the wretched London Live but then something of a home for good music and the musicians that made it. They offered him his début radio session, and he gladly accepted.

Given the first single's lack of impact, it was deemed sensible to mark the release of David's album, *A Century Ends*, by another – and the choice was its previously mentioned opening track, 'Shine'. Robin Millar would contribute guitar to the track, having been present at the initial Town House recording session. "He played on those three demo songs that we did before the full album, one of which is 'Shine' which is why he appeared on that," the producer confirmed.

Dave Anderson, who also supplied piano, Wurlitzer piano and Hammond organ, had worked with drummer Steve Sidelnyk on a previous Aztec Camera project. Rob Holden also knew him so he was in from the start. Session bass player Mark Smith was a respected regular on the London session scene, while Neill MacColl, son of folk icon Ewan and half-brother of singer-songwriter Kirsty (who would tragically lose her life in a late 2000 boating accident), would prove an able lieutenant. He had played the role before in The Bible, accompanying another promising singer-songwriter in Boo Hewardine, while other critically acclaimed ventures in which he'd been involved included The Liberty Horses. "Neill was an accomplished player and writer in his own right. I can't quite remember how he came in on the act. I think we were just looking around for a second guitarist and someone suggested him."

Anderson himself came into the project on the back of an Edwyn Collins album, *Hell Bent On Compromise*, and production work with Black, the one-man band also known as Colin Vearncombe who'd scored such Eighties hits as 'It's A Wonderful Life' and 'Sweetest Smile'. There's a line of progression between Black, Collins and Gray that suggests Anderson was seen as someone to get the most out of a singer-songwriter.

"Well it's one of my bags, I suppose," he says. "We got on because we listen to a lot of the same sort of music: Tom Waits, Bob Dylan, Van Morrison, the sort of stuff that you can obviously hear in Dave's music at that time. But it was really the start of my production career. I'd been a studio engineer at the Power Plant and was looking to do as much production work as I could, so it was a heaven-sent opportunity."

When *A Century Ends* appeared in June 1993, comparisons from critics and fans veered between major influences Dylan and The Waterboys, the latter because of what *Q* called "bulgy-veined balladry, ornate lyrics and a noticeable Celtic feel." The cover, they noted rather sourly, featured David "looking like a First World War poet." Certainly the head and shoulders mugshot with no-nonsense, reversed out white capitals proclaiming title and artist brooked no nonsense.

The template he took into the recording process was *Nebraska*, Bruce Springsteen's stark solo effort from 1982. "This album is just one man and an acoustic guitar in a bathroom," he told *Mojo*. "It's sheer brilliance, so revealing. The recording quality's not great but it just doesn't matter. I'm fascinated by him; he's a great writer. His great obsession is people who are hard-done by; it's their wanting to live and be free but not knowing quite how to do it that gets them into trouble. It's a very innocent thing, but they suddenly end up in a dark place where they've got hard decisions to make. He's fuckin' clever; all the time he just leads people to an image and then hits them with it. It's a staggering record."

For Dave Anderson, the challenge was to retain what made Gray "a fantastic solo performer – that was what we tried to get onto the record. A lot of it was done very live, vocals and everything, just live in the studio really."

'Shine' kicked off the album in more or less exactly the same basic, strummy way as 'Birds Without Wings'. Again there were landscape references, this time a shoreline where he and his summer love could take one last walk together. The vibrato of the first single was now more of a guttural, Dylanesque drawl, modest piano and a Garth Hudson-style organ behind the acoustic guitar underscoring the comparison. For producer Anderson, 'Shine' set the tone for the whole effort, "because, as I explained, it was one of the first batch of three songs we recorded before the album and it was, if you like, the first confirmation that we really could make a special record. It's a great vocal performance and the music was just what I was looking for in terms of the stripped down approach and atmosphere."

The title track, 'A Century Ends', would be released as a single-song radio promo to promote the album's US release via Virgin Records' Caroline subsidiary (though this event was still five months distant). One wonders what the Yanks made of it, as it's fairly downbeat stuff about "Anger spilling out like gasoline" as a self-absorbed society "admires its own reflection". Not exactly breakfast show on WABC material... but the musical setting, the verse melodically reminiscent of Cat Stevens' 'First Cut Is The Deepest', drove the point home. Sidelnyk in particular did a sterling job on drums behind Anderson's keyboards, Paul Brady again a reference point.

'Debauchery' lived up to its title as Gray, "a lonely man with five bottles of wine to share" found himself "badly in need of an afternoon's debauuuuuu-cheree". The deed was done as a hailstorm tumbles and the rail line rumbles and we're left none the wiser as the outcome of the affair: 'Lay Lady Lay' it wasn't, but real life it clearly was.

For whatever reason, by chance or otherwise, the lyrics of 'Let The Truth Sting' faced a picture of Gray in the CD booklet wearing a bucket on his head. This was certainly a page full of thoughts – too many to digest at one sitting, perhaps, as Gray railed against "this empire of dust" with "a river of words". Somehow the lack of a conventional chorus made this rather relentlessly strummy, and by the end of it the listener would have done well to remember exactly what it is the singer was complaining about.

The gentle 'Gathering Dust' found the young man musing on his uncertain future to the economical backing of his own acoustic guitar and MacColl's 'Maggie May'-style mandolin. The hook, a singalong 'Na na na' chorus, distracted attention from some somewhat clichéd lyrics. This was Dave Anderson's other highlight, "because it was just a great moment in the studio – we recorded all together, vocals as well, just sat round in a semi-circle."

The album's mid-point songs, 'Wisdom' and 'Lead Me Upstairs', would by coincidence be those that survived to grace David's late Nineties stage set. Indeed, a version of the latter, recorded live, would appear on the B-side of breakthrough single 'Babylon's original 1998 release by IHT. MacColl's almost dissonant lead guitar embellished a strummed acoustic as Gray told the tale of another brief liaison with a woman who was "dark inside. . . she asked me for the truth and all I did was lied."

'Living Room' was the second consecutive track on the album (the other being the fade of 'Lead Me Upstairs') to feature a brief contribution from saxophonist Michael Smith. The line about last night being "just a blur through a head full of beer" was one many listeners could empathise with. If life was a living room, said Gray, then "I'm in the hall and I'm glad." Ever the outsider, then. . .

David's first single 'Birds Without Wings' was tucked away as the penultimate track as if its obligatory inclusion were somehow resented. In fact it's a song Gray has looked back and marvelled on and is by no means out of place here. Maybe that's surprising since, as previously mentioned, it had either been recorded earlier on one of the other demo sessions or (Dave Anderson suspects, a decade later) came from another session of recordings. All the other tracks save 'Shine' were done in a two-week spell at Town House 3, then mixed at Battery Studios in Willesden. The Power Plant studios were closing at the time, and didn't figure in the equation.

'A Century Ends' was brought to a close, appropriately, by 'It's All Over', which more or less continued the introspective mood of 'Birds'. David had "Beer in his head" again, too much this time, and the long white road lay unfolded before him. "I can't think straight" was his befuddled conclusion. This would often conclude the live set, too.

Looking back at his first album on VH1 some years later, Gray stated his aims in recording had been simple and straightforward: "I just wanted to make a record and put everything into it. The chance to emulate the people you admired I suppose is what you were looking at. The rest of it was a mystery to me. I didn't have an opinion about how the industry worked out what would be the best marketing ploy or how to break the record. It was all such a new experience.

"I thought I had a recording philosophy. It worked in certain places but I had so much to learn. I remember thinking the record was going to go out there and knock them dead. I only hoped that it would be given the chance."

VH1's website certainly reviewed it favourably. "*A Century Ends* earns David Gray a reputation as a Welsh-accented Bob Dylan. The comparison is fitting, given both singers' penchant for plaintive, poetic lyrics and powerful balladry. Unlike Dylan, though, David Gray possesses a voice that is exceptionally warm and inviting. From the solemn 'Gathering Dust' to more upbeat rockers like 'Wisdom,' *Century* showcases the young Gray's vocal versatility as well as his gift for clever wordplay. Backed mainly by acoustic guitar, Gray infuses each song on this début with passion and intelligence, hinting at a promising career ahead."

At the time, producer Dave Anderson was as frustrated as his charge at the lack of impact the album made. "I don't think the label knew what to do with it, to be honest. At that time, singer songwriters were as unfashionable as they could possibly be and I don't think they knew how to promote it — so they didn't!"

Hut's press releases of the time were drawing comparisons, a trifle desperately, with American Music Club's Mark Eitzel and Miracle Legion's Mark Mulcachy. "He's not out to make you feel comfortable, though his tactics are frequently subtle and the results often joyous." *Vox* magazine at least laid off the comparisons, giving him a mention as "A perfectly balanced singer-songwriter... with a chip on both shoulders!"

Gray responded rather obliquely to the label in the *Irish Sunday Press*. "Do I have even one chip? I'm sure I have a few. That's what young people are like. It's almost like a rite of passage, or something. But I don't think I'm particularly chippish!"

Amused or not by such wordplay, David Gray himself was desperate to avoid a 'folkie' tag. "The folk thing... I don't know about it, I don't know what's going on there at all. I don't feel very akin to it; I have a different sensibility. I'm as much an indie kid as I am a folkie – I mean, that's my youth – so I've been affected by all kinds of different things, and they all come out in different ways. I'm in loads of traditions – it's the hallmark of anybody who's any good at anything. In my opinion it's the hallmark of any good artist. If they're not dealing with what's wrong with things – the lamentable things of life – what the fuck are they dealing with? So it's not just folk, it's punk – punk was a statement of that disaffection, but it was more a frustrated cry than a constructive one asking for some change in the ongoing march of multi-nationalism and alienation that everyone suffers from."

Call it what you will, David's début album would remain frustratingly out of print for several years after he severed connections with Hut – but those who managed to track down copies have found that, rather than having developed dramatically away from his first musical footstep, *A Century Ends* was far from obsolete. His conversational songwriting style and surprising maturity drew the listener in further to a world that one critic termed "pretty dark stuff – broken relationships, futility, mindless hedonism...". The ten tracks were remarkably consistent in their portrayal of emotion and even though the production was occasionally a little liberal the songs shone through.

An anonymous reviewer from Galway, Ireland gave a fan's perspective on amazon.com when the record was finally re-released in summer 2001. "This album was David's first and, in most fans' opinion, his best. Powerful poetic lyrics make this album mysterious in the fact that David Gray took another 10 (actually five, but who's count-ing?) years to break through. If you own *White Ladder* you simply have to buy this album to see where Gray started and to hear him at his best."

'Shine', the radio-friendly opening track and second single, would become the key to creating his cult following in Ireland, not least because it titled an album by home-grown chanteuse Mary Black. At the time, however, it never became the hit it should have been. (DJ Donal Dineen would later seize on it and it was its exposure on his *No Disco* programme that would be the catalyst to Gray's popularity in the Emerald Isle.)

The two B-sides that accompanied its release as a single in March 1993 were also worth lending an ear to. 'Brick Walls' was compara-tively lush compared with the bleakness of many Gray singles tracks, with emphatically conventional instrumentation including drums. Like so many of his songs, the title appeared as an afterthought rather than a chorus as such, though it was repeated often enough as the track faded. His vocal here was reminiscent of another Mancunian, Mick Hucknall, with just a dash of an unlikely third – the Fall's Mark E Smith. 'The Rice', by contrast, was back to strictly solo mode, def-initely and clearly enunciated lyrics being semi-spoken over an almost Paul Simon-esque chord progression. The curious use of kitchen terminology (broccoli, fridge, spatula) predated the current vogue of TV cooks, or you could well have heard this embroidering a Jamie Oliver documentary. A mandolin or higher-stringed guitar played a second part as the song progressed. The title 'The Rice' seemed somewhat obscure given the song's hook, "under the hem of the night", but the declamation "Let the rice burn/It cannot deter my love for you" had a strange power. Gray had the chef, naked or otherwise, clearly in his sights.

The three-tracker headed by 'Shine' would be followed by a third and final single selection in 'Wisdom', released in June. This would be well received live, when it usually appeared as an encore, but on first hearing sounded like an acoustic rehash of Chip Taylor's 'Wild Thing' – the famous three-chord trick beloved of Jimi Hendrix, the Troggs et al. Electric guitars now reinforced the strumming acoustic, while the declaimed listing of things that were "no good to me any more"

– time, wisdom and patience – would account for its popularity as an audience participation song.

The B-sides were once again omitted from the finished album, and would all become sought-after by fans until the arrival of an EP collection in 2001. Meanwhile, the miracle of technology would make these available on the world wide web as MP3s for anyone with the patience and ability to seek them out. 'Lovers' was a very bare-boned declamatory love song that again sounded remarkably like a Lindisfarne track – especially when the slide guitar entered the fray over bass and minimal percussion. It had the feel of someone trying to hold on to a feeling while knowing "by next summertime we'll have (maybe) forgotten it all."

By contrast, '4AM' was a track with a band feel, introduced with acoustic guitar and tambourine before a dominant bass piano figure grabs the attention. By the middle section an organ had appeared as David continued his journey through the hours of the day. His deep vocal tones sound a ringer for Joan Armatrading here as he declaims 'the cruellest thing that I have ever known/time and circumstance taking their toll'. Altogether, this was a moody and magnificent performance, if the meaning of it all remained somewhat obscure.

Having achieved his lifelong ambition and made a record, David Gray could not rest on his laurels. The album now had to be promoted with every ounce of effort in his body. There was every chance of the States taking to him, so plans were made to ship him out there under the Virgin Records umbrella, release of the album having been scheduled by their Caroline subsidiary.

He was originally hooked up with Maria McKee, former singer of new country/punk fusionists Lone Justice, who had scored a UK chart-topper with 'Show Me Heaven' (the theme to hit film *Days Of Thunder*) in 1990 but was finding it increasingly difficult to follow up. Other claims to fame the singer could boast included being stepsister to Love's Bryan McLean (who penned that band's classic 'Aloneagainor') and that her extrovert stage demeanour had encouraged Deacon Blue's Ricky Ross to pen his own hit, 'Real Gone Kid'.

In the autumn of 1993 she'd set off on a tour of the US and Canada promoting her latest album *You Gotta Sin To Get Saved*, a raucous affair, produced by Black Crowes alumnus George Drakoulias - and

David Gray was selected as the opening act. The exposure was timely, and his début in the US would bring an unexpected bonus in the shape of a kindred musical spirit. He became friends with McKee backing musician David Nolté, and the pair ended up playing together a couple of times before the tour was over.

Multi-instrumentalist Nolté, who was in his thirties and so significantly older than David, had a bit of a history in West Coast music terms, having been one of three Los Angeles brothers who'd formed seminal indie band The Last in 1976. They had released early singles on their own label, Backlash but had signed to Bomp! by the time of their first and most notable album, *LA Explosion* (1979). He left in 1985 to join anglophile outfit Wednesday Week (named after a song by Irish punk pioneers The Undertones), switching from bass to guitar as he did so, but returned to The Last four years later to make a cameo appearance on 'Awakenings'. Wednesday Week had featured a lead vocalist called Kristi Callan, who would later become Mrs David Nolté, and who would also enter the David Gray picture in future months.

Now a musician and freelance graphic designer in Los Angeles, David Nolté recalls how impressed he was with David Gray the solo performer. "He had me from the first song I saw him play. . . huge voice, great songs, really into what he was doing, tons of confidence, great influences. I played live with him during that Maria McKee tour a couple of times before getting to record with him."

Nolté was familiar with *A Century Ends*, but felt Gray was already adding dimensions to the compositions in performance. "I had grown used to hearing those songs played on tour with just Dave and sometimes Dave and Neill (MacColl) and I think I preferred those versions to what's on the first CD. The CD still holds up today. . . it's just that live these songs were more powerful."

Touring the States, such a long-held ambition, was one that would quickly sour for David Gray when he tried solo dates, cut adrift with "a rental car and a credit card" and fending for himself. Not very well, as it turned out. On one memorable occasion, he managed to spend up to his credit limit in Los Angeles, leaving himself with no means to fulfil a show that same night near San Diego, 90 miles away. Having managed to beg and borrow enough funds for a plane ticket and a taxi to the venue, he was just about to congratulate himself on making the venue in time – only to find he was the only one who had.

"The place was dead empty," Gray says. "I'd come all this way, fought and struggled. I felt like a hero just showing up, and I get there – no one's around. When you work so hard and you're just not getting anywhere, it's hard to avoid this feeling of absolute irrelevance – the sheer pointlessness of it all." Though a gig was scheduled for the next night, in Arizona, he simply didn't have the stomach for it. "I called the agent, said the car broke down. I bought a bottle of wine and went to the beach. It was like, 'What the fuck am I doing?'"

Only one musician that assisted on *A Century Ends* would make it onto the road with David. Neil MacColl would come along on a few of the tours until the end of 1994. (The most high profile of his early collaborators would turn out to be drummer Sidelnyk. Having played with the likes of R.E.M. and Richard Ashcroft, he spent 2001 on tour with Madonna, no less.) MacColl, meanwhile, was also still around when he went back into the studio to record his second album, *Flesh*.

A Hut Records biography of this time had stressed that "David Gray's remarkable singing and songwriting are more than just personal visions. Far from being locked in a personal; struggle with his own demons, his music has the power to touch anyone's innermost thoughts – if only they let it."

The importance of these last five words was soon to be tested.

CHAPTER 3

The Flesh Is Weak

In 1993, David married trainee solicitor Olivia in Los Angeles. The Maria McKee tour had just finished, and it was a brief window of opportunity before he became too firmly embroiled in the business of making his 'difficult' second album. "It was in one of these dodgy wedding chapels," he'd later recall. "This ridiculous character married us. But it was brilliant getting married, a fantastic occasion." It was a quiet ceremony, so quiet that he managed to get himself booked for a gig on his wedding night – which he apparently played! His bride could hardly have been mollified by a 'Special thanks' credit on the sleeve of *Flesh*, released in September 1994, since she shared it with the musicians, producer and record label. . .

While singer-songwriters are known to thrive on angst and isolation, David doesn't see his own creative process working that way – "The ordeal that is living is exactly the same. The entire weight of our suffering day to day, if you want to get involved in it, remains identical" – so the danger of such domestic bliss stifling his muse was slim. On the other hand, who could blame him for wanting to tell the world how he felt about his new-found happiness?

As you'd expect his state of mind was very much reflected in a record whose ornate sleeve marked it from the outset as a radical departure from its predecessor. A monochrome picture of David – the same one that would be used for the 2001 *EPs 92–94* release – sat among a batch of posed portraits in a photographer's window. A credit suggested the assistance of Stoke Newington Photo Studios; at any event, the reissue of *Flesh* in July 2001 was in a considerably less ornate black and white sleeve, the original image relegated to the inside back cover.

The intention had been to throw off the image he had acquired, against his will, of the "serious geezer". "[It] wasn't really that representative, but it's sort of inevitable," he said. "You're gonna get portrayed as something, so if people figure you're a miserable fucker then that's the way it's gonna be!"

The cover of *A Century Ends*, he said, had been "all too serious. I got kind of stitched up." Hence the bright, colourful cover? "Yeah, that was my idea." This time around, he'd still be raging "but *for* things, though, not against."

Marriage immersed him in a whole new social circle since, by his own admission, he had neglected to keep in touch with anyone from childhood days in Solva. "I've got a whole bunch of friends now in London. I think friends are very important. I think it's something I'm started to realise a few years ago, that I was missing out on a very valuable thing in my kind of solo existence.

"I don't know why it is, but it's a quirk of mine that I don't seem to be very good at keeping the friendship thing going. I tend to move on and be thinking different thoughts. I can be in a completely different place. I mean, I moved around a lot and, when I got married, I fell in with a new bunch of people that my wife knew. So that was like starting all over again with a new bunch of people."

It wasn't the only thing that was different. When David returned from a tour of Europe to record his second album, things had changed behind the scenes. Where once it wore the transient trappings of an independent label (though funded by a major), Hut Records had, by this time, been fully integrated into the Virgin empire. His music would henceforth be a product of Vernon's Yard Recordings, named after Virgin's original offices situated off the quaint Portobello Road street market in West London.

Quaint, however, is not the word you'd use to describe David's situation. Though Hut still released him in Europe, Virgin now controlled his recording and production, signing him to a new contract that included no provision for singles, just one LP. Soon afterwards, the A&R man who'd signed him left, and with him went the freedom David had enjoyed with Hut as it had been.

In fairness, evidence on paper still didn't suggest Mr Gray was living up to 'Next Big Thing' status. Despite subsequent flattering comparisons to Dylan's *Blonde On Blonde* and Springsteen's *Nebraska* (again), almost all coloured by hindsight's pink-tinged spectacles, *A Century Ends* had hardly set the charts alight: UK sales are reckoned to have been in the region of 2,000 copies. Little wonder he wasn't top of his new label's priority list.

"Nobody was interested," said Hut founder Dave Boyd of his first album. "I mean *nobody*. David was beating his head against the wall; *I* was beating my head against the wall." Hopefully, that painful experience would be alleviated by the new effort, whose dramatically increased instrumentation would make it more of a mainstream affair.

That hope, however, would be dashed by circumstance – and when David Nolté got a call from Gray's manager asking if he could come to England to record for a couple of weeks, it was the sign of things going wrong. "I got a tape of the songs he was working on, took them with me on a tour of Japan with Maria McKee and then flew home, repacked and went straight to London to record. We spent a day rehearsing then two weeks recording."

According to Nolté, Gray had already completed more recording with the personnel he had used on his first album and wasn't all that happy with the results. This is where Nolté re-entered the picture and new drummer Craig McClune (universally known as Clune) took his bow. A very early David Gray gig had seen him support Clune's band at the Wag Club in London in 1990. As with Nolté, they hit it off and remained in touch. Clune would not only turn out to be an excellent musical ally, being able to turn his hand to several other instruments as well as supplying harmony vocals, but would prove a bit of a showman on stage, adding a much-needed second visual focus to the 'star'. (His penchant for gaudy, Hawaiian-style shirts certainly helped in this respect!)

This album would represent a marked departure from his début, not least because of the personnel involved. Other unfamiliar names in the frame included Andy Metcalfe, originally of Cambridge cult band The Soft Boys and latterly with Squeeze, contributed Hammond organ, while there was also an alternate rhythm section to Clune and Nolté in the shape of Simon Edwards (bass) and Roy Dodds (drums), both of whom had previously played with chart-toppers Fairground Attraction of 'Perfect' fame. Neill MacColl would have been aware of the pair through his connection with Eddi Reader, the former Fairground Attraction singer who'd become a regular collaborator with his former Bible-mate Boo Hewerdine

But it was the Clune/Nolté rhythm section that clearly pointed the way to the future. Appearing on three and five of the album's ten tracks respectively, they offered Gray the chance of a stable backing unit. "He found Clune, called me and used his collaborator at the time, Neill MacColl," the bassist recalls. "We clicked as a band and had a great time recording. The out-takes from these recordings (which have yet to be aired) are as good if not better than the record. Anyway, when they put everything together for the CD, half the stuff was from these sessions and half from the previous sessions." Interestingly, you'll look in vain on *Flesh* for a production credit. Dave Anderson's services had not been retained, for reasons that were never explained to him. "That's something you'd better ask David!" he laughed in 2001, having since happily consolidated his own production career with acts like The Sundays as well as starting his own record label, Fidela, with Andy Cox from The Beat and Fine Young Cannibals.

"We were due to carry on, and it was very disappointing from my point of view that he decided basically to go in and do it himself with an engineer." Having had guidance for his first time in a state-of-the art studio, Armstrong believes Gray felt he now knew enough to get by and wanted to take it further. "There's a lot of artists make their first record with a producer, then it's 'I know how to do that now so I'll do it myself.'" That's exactly how it seemed to be. Jim Abiss, who'd been credited as engineer for *A Century Ends*, was retained in that role and, with Gray and MacColl, took an active hand in the mixing process.*

---

* He would, like David Gray, change musical direction in the future, scoring several chart hits with dance act DJ Shadow in the mid 1990s as well as enjoying success with US indie group The Sneaker Pimps.

From David Nolté's viewpoint Gray ultimately produced himself, even if the credit was missing. "Neill, Jim Abiss and Dave were the three in charge of production but Dave had veto power. Any time someone would try to push him in a direction he wasn't sure of or keen on, he would dig in and say no until they would listen. On the other hand, all of us were asked our opinions and there were suggestions made from Clune and myself that ended up on the record."

Gray himself made some interesting observations to Irish journalist Colin Harper when asked if he feared other people tampering with his work? "Yeah. . . though 'fear' isn't quite the right word. I've a mistrust of 'production'. I prefer to capture things as nakedly and as live as they can be, but I'm realising that you do need a person in the studio who's studio wise, to make the most of the situation because it's not live, it's a foreign environment. I'm not someone to stick around and fiddle with mixes – after a couple of hours in the studio I'm gone. . ."

He was already looking to change his songwriting tack from *A Century Ends*. It wasn't even that conscious a decision," he explained to Harper. "I didn't feel like continuing in that vein. I wrote songs about what was happening to me, which was far more important to me than the rest of the world was – living life through your own self. So I saw that if I could encapsulate the forces of hope, I suppose, and renew all that I'd experienced, then that would probably be the most potent kind of thing I could put onto tape – far more potent than a kind of rage against a general thing.

"It was a specific thing – lots of the songs on the first album were very broad. Not that I think there's anything wrong with that, it's just that I've changed and my perspective now is more on an intimate scale. I feel more confident [dealing] with stuff that I know I've gone through rather than sort of attacking a void, which I don't actually know. It's like you find much more than the simple issues when you go into real situations. They're far more complicated and apathy is only one cog, you know. So I'd rather try and discuss, in a song, an actual situation, throwing beams of light out of it that are encroaching on it or revealed by it. And I feel that the world that's revealed through that is more convincing. I don't like to use the words 'light and dark', but it's got a kind of upbeat quality."

Asked if he'd discovered more personal contentment since the last record, he admitted this was true – "and that reflects in the work. I mean, it would be stupid to continue these 'tirades' when the scope of your life is expanding in a different direction – not that it cuts you off from the outside world, but it's just you've got more to deal with. It's far more elaborate than your life was previously."

Flesh was ready for release by the end of March 1994, yet for reasons unknown to the artist himself, sat six months on the stocks before finally seeing the light of day in September. "They come up with weird reasons to delay it, like there's too much pollen in the air to put it out!" One silver lining was the fact that, when the second album from David Gray was finally released by the Hut label, it received simultaneous North American issue on Caroline. It was always going to face an uphill struggle to survive on its own merits in a marketplace where singles were the current currency, yet its excellence soon started a word of mouth going that marked him out as a singer-songwriter of some promise.

Tony Clayton Lea, like Colin Harper an Irish-based journalist who contributed to *Mojo* magazine, was so smitten he immediately placed it in his Top 10 albums of the year, allowing that though "David Gray sings about pretty much the same stuff as everyone else (love, hurt), he expresses these better than many of his contemporaries. . . believeable, emotional stuff."

While so many writers peak with their first album, using the cream of their output from the unsigned years and find themselves unable to turn the creative tap on again when caught on the album-tour-album promotional treadmill, inspiration for David Gray hadn't been hard to come by. "I was all fired up and into my music at the time," he'd recall. "I had fallen in love and got married, and a lot of the songs were about that."

If only the making of the album had been as straightforward as he makes it sound! From the outset, the sessions were fraught with outside interference. "The record company turned round and said, 'You haven't got much money left, you'd better get your album finished.' We hadn't even started – it was all a bit of a mess." It's a tribute, then, to David's abilities and persistence that *Flesh* turned out as well as it did. Indeed, it remains many long-time fans' favourite.

When quizzed by Colin Harper later in the year, Gray insisted he hadn't been forced to compromise – yet – but admitted to "an unspoken pressure, which has prevailed a little bit, but you can't help it. You need a lot of experience to override pressure like that; you need a lot of confidence in what you do and what works best." *Flesh*, he believed, had "flashes. . . it's got some really good stuff on it. I'd say it got closer to the live thing than the last one did."

Lyrics continued to form the backbone of his appeal, but while admitting that "words is what I'm into," he insisted that "to get further into words doesn't necessarily mean using more of them. I see that economy is all. You can say a lot with a few sentences. A bluesman can put a lot of suffering into a few clichés, but if he sings them right and maybe just tweaks the odd word in here or there – a weird word that you wouldn't expect – suddenly you've got this kind of classic. . . They don't extend their word play very far. Generally it's pretty restricted, apart from the odd Howlin' Wolf number where you get this 'diamonds in the sand' kind of weird imagery."

Q magazine's four-star review highlighted the opening 'What Are You?' as '*Flesh*'s key cut, deeming it "invigoratingly angry. . . he fumes about pop stars who sideline artistic purity for the sake of loads of money. Yeah! Bastards!" Certainly the accusatory lyrics are delivered over layers of raucous electric and acoustic guitars, a "spittle-flecked folk-grunge hybrid" in Q-speak and a development from the previous album's acoustic feel.* This would also be the first Gray fans would have heard of Clune, whose percussion pushed the accusing singer – "You lost your spine!" – to the limit.

The song, he'd reveal, "was quite an old one" and placed at the start of the album "'cos it's more kind of relative to what's gone before. . . I'm not going to say it's the 'end' of anything, but after that one things set off apace, (we're) into the new direction. It didn't fit on the album very well, but it's just one of those things." It had been based on no-one in particular but "probably to do with myself. It could have been aimed inwards at a certain point in time. It's such a straight-ahead riff that, I mean, it had to be a pretty basic idea. So it's got a very simple structure and it's very aggressive. It's not something I stand by all the

---

* In concert, it took the place of the similarly feisty 'Let The Truth Sting'.

time, but it's a good one to do live, specially if the audience is crap – then you aim it at them!"

Next up came another live favourite 'The Light' that, by dint of continuous performance and refinement, had metamorphosed from the B-side it had originally been into something rather more ambitious. Instrumentally, Iggy Pop/Madness sideman Seamus Beaghen's piano added a Van Morrison-esque feel ("Here come the night", David vamped across the closing coda in homage to Morrison's Sixties group Them), while Neill Maccoll's mandolin solo provided welcome mid-song relief. The effect was impressive: a leap towards Gray's future sound without sacrificing any of his trademark vocal intensity.

Track three, 'Coming Down', had more than a touch of Fairground Attraction about it, and not just due to the subtle presence of the Edwards/Dodds rhythm section: maybe it was the unusual sound of the autoharp. That exotic instrument would not be featured live, where the song would grow and develop over time. "Took too much powder to sleep" marked Gray's first drug reference, predating 'Babylon's "chemicals in my bloodstream", while the song's instrumental play-out failed to prepare the listener for what came next as he cut back to an intimate piano and vocal delivery.

Track four, 'Falling Free', was typical of the songs reflecting the new love in the writer's life. A starkly beautiful ballad (the first time Gray had featured majorly on keyboards in a recording), it exposed his vulnerable side every bit as much as anything on his debut release. Though critical of the album as a whole, David exempted this track: "Some of it worked out well, 'Falling Free' I'm still very fond of." He likened the approach to the performance as "like a demo session", and the simplicity of the setting certainly let the song's beauty shine through.

There's no secret as to who he was crediting with opening up the door to his soul. "I don't remember ever feeling this way before," he confessed before concluding that they should "trust it all to chance" and enjoy the moment. A version of this song, recorded live, would appear on the B-side of 'Babylon's original 1998 release on his own IHT label.

'Made Up My Mind', like 'What Are You?' and 'Love's Old Song', saw Gray plugging in and coming closer to rocking out than on his previous album. He was moving ahead, not lagging behind, putting on a positive face, but there was a feeling of more heat than light being generated. With Clune's percussion pushing ever onwards and lyrics with more than a few suspect rhymes, 'Made Up My Mind' was probably a song for live performance rather than inner contemplation. The next selection, though, would start with purely guitar and vocals, building with a touch of slide guitar before the final verse saw the rhythm section join the fray.

The title, 'The Mystery Of Love', could almost be from John Martyn or another romance-besotted folkie. But to David Gray, the love to which he was referring encompassed an affair with the capital city that would become his home as much as the woman he had chosen as his life partner. "I fell in love with a tower block in the middle of London, surrounded by London and all its madness," he explained. "I had a brilliant time because I went down there, got a record deal, and then I, like, fell in love, got married and all that stuff." This, then, was clearly the most autobiographical song on a self-revealing album.

While others had in the past bemoaned the cruel 'Streets Of London', David's 'Mystery Of Love' was more upbeat. "I used to find it quite alien when I went down before I lived there, but I never really had a bad experience there. But I can see how alien it can be, it's a cold place in so many ways." As for leaving the girl in the tower block behind as he circled the country in search of fame and fortune, "It's one of the hardest things about the job."

'Lullaby' reverted to the minimal approach of the first album with David on solo guitar, ending on quite a nifty guitar riff: "Hear the bells!" David instructed as he played out, having welcomed the dawn and consigned the past night to history. The song was credited as having been recorded by him, suggesting a one-off demo performance that couldn't be bettered in a more formal environment: either way, like 'Falling Free', it supplied a welcome change of style and pace.

Dropping the pessimism, 'New Horizons' had a sense of change and a broadening of his world view that permeated much of the album. Over chord changes reminiscent of Joan Armatrading, he declaimed that "love will find its own direction". Life was opening up before his very eyes, and the joy was one he wanted to share.

Penultimate track 'Love's Old Song' is undoubtedly the one moment of his recording past David Gray would like to erase. As it is, he has to fast-forward through it. "That haunts me to this day. People come up to me saying 'I love 'Love's Old Song', it's one of my favourites' and I'm 'Jesus Christ, I don't know what to say. Good. I'm glad somebody does'." It is all a bit noisy and pub-rocky, similar to Graham Parker's late-Seventies output, and with David giving it a "Yeh yeh" and a "woh-oh" you almost expect a horn section to join in the fun, along with the kitchen sink. "Ridiculous bar-room rock," he said in March 2001, nominating it as the worst record he'd ever made. A harsh judgement, but certainly one of the lesser tracks.

Few albums leave the title song until last, but then David Gray is no ordinary writer. Another stark intro underlined the fact that *Flesh* had been an album of sonic extremes rather than consistency. But he clearly was, in the words of the track, intent on putting flesh on the bones of his dreams. Interestingly, when Colin Harper challenged him as to what those bones were, the answer came: "I don't know. . . It could be my 'dreams' for the world. . ."

VH1 was reasonably complimentary about the result, while agreeing that he had yet to find a truly individual voice. "As on his debut album, the mostly understated production and straightforward instrumentation of *Flesh* complements Gray's intimate songwriting style. His soulful, heavily-accented vocal delivery invites comparisons to Van Morrison and Mike Scott of The Waterboys."

As ever, though, the artist's high standards of quality control would consign *Flesh* to the dustbin of history. "The album hasn't got a consistency to it," he'd later complain to VH1, while admitting that he liked "elements of the acoustic sound and the more understated things like 'Falling Free'. But then there's other bits and bobs, things that don't really work well in my opinion." In 2001, he went further, exonerating the songs while condemning the performances. "I think that, by and large, it's a little messy. I should have spent longer getting it right. I like some of the songs on there, I don't know why I don't play them so much. I like 'Falling Free', and (there's) some other good ones on there."

Bassist David Nolté has remained convinced that, despite a difficult gestation period, *Flesh* is a more than worthwhile album. "My opinion of the album both then and now is that it's a great record. It may not be the most cohesive thing he's done but there are a handful of tracks that still sound great today: 'What Are You?', 'The Light' and 'Falling Free' stand out for me. The *Flesh* record had a few different moods than *A Century Ends*. He was trying a lot of different things probably not wanting to repeat himself. But Dave has told me that this is his least favourite."

Reviews at the time would be thin on the ground. Q, the hip listener's bible, made it wait behind the better-known likes of Prince, Sinead O'Connor and R.E.M. before giving it four stars out of five. America's *Alternative Press* also approved of an "explosive, often solo-acoustic-waged war of words. Closer to that celebrated Celtic interloper Mike Scott than Scott's spiritual dad, Van Morrison. . . Gray's caustic rasp is nevertheless telling." They also spotted "some Van the Man trademarks, the quiet bits where David rambles on, and some lyrical play that could have come from Dylan Thomas' *Under Milk Wood*."

Vox's Lisa Verrico granted it a generous eight out of ten, believing it to be "essential listening for anyone who feels life is a constant, soul-searching struggle. . . Gray's songwriting skills have clearly moved on for the simpler structure of former single 'Shine', though lyrically he remains obsessed by frustration, futility and fear."

Although it was received well by those critics who cared to give it column inches, the album failed to make any real commercial noise in a chart dominated by the likes of Wet Wet Wet's *Greatest Hits*, *Definitely Maybe*, the incendiary début album from Oasis and, of all things, *The Three Tenors in Concert*. This lack of impact was also partially due to continuing problems at the record label which led to no singles being released. Even though only 'The Light' and 'Coming Down' would find a place in his regular live set, many fans still regard *Flesh* as the best David Gray album.

Typical of these is Casey Quintin from the United States, who believes "This is the album that *should* have started it all. It's an album filled with stories of a tortured man and lost soul. . . Talking to himself, it seems, Gray finds all of his faults, (or maybe the faults of the world?) With fire in his voice, he's a man searching for an answer. Then there are the songs of love, where he takes on a much different persona. Just by listening to him, you can see the calm in his eyes, the steadiness of his hands, and you can hear the soul in his words. This album goes from rage to love, back to that anger and then to a redeeming ending note. A very diverse album."

In Britain, in 1994, the diverse David Gray was fighting a losing battle – not helped when Hut put him on an autumn tour with Liverpool's Ian McNabb, once frontman of The Icicle Works. McNabb's crowd, he concluded, "were just not interested at all", though he had time for the man himself. "He's all right, he's a nice guy – but we didn't have a very good tour. It was crap. It wasn't my tour – I was supporting. I can't go out on my own yet. I haven't got enough fans." This had come on the back of a stuttering Phoenix appearance where Gray had failed to make any impact on the serried ranks of festival-goers.

As with The Kinks, David decided to go out on a limb with The Icicle Works crowd, preferring any reaction to none at all. "I really had a go at a couple of the audiences," he told Q magazine. "What do you think I'm fucking here for? You're here to fucking listen to music, so why don't you shut up and listen to me? Of course they were out to have a pint and listen to Ian McNabb, and there was this man with spiky hair shouting at them. It didn't work."

As things weren't happening at home, David widened his word view and decided another visit to the home of the singer-songwriter, the US of A, would be his next step. But this time he would not travel alone. His first taste of the Stateside highways and byways would be in the company of American country/roots chanteuse Shawn Colvin, who at 37 would, like Gray, find pop stardom comparatively late in life. Her first album *Steady On* had appeared in 1990 and surprisingly but pleasingly took a folk Grammy, while 1993's *Fat City* had picked up a nomination alongside the mega-diva trio of Whitney Houston, Mariah Carey and Tina Turner.

Since sales did not yet match those of her fellow nominees for Best Pop Vocal Performance, Ms Colvin was propelled onto a ten-week tour, for which David was the show opener. "It was very low on luxury, that tour," he recalls – but at least, unlike the Auteurs jaunt, he wasn't following the bus! The soundtrack for the tour was *Banjonique*, the 1994 comeback album by Sixties banjo pioneer Walt Koken, and David recalls "a lot of air banjo being played" during those ten weeks. *Banjonique* can apparently be recommended. "It's the best banjo record ever, fantastic for mellow, off-your-head moments in the back of the bus."

Opening for Colvin at least guaranteed him a crowd (presumably there was no repeat of his Joan Baez-baiting antics). And she continued on an upward spiral, thanks to the impetus of her tour and an album of cover versions that followed. But the *Frampton Comes Alive* scenario – play to millions, they buy your album and hey presto, you're a millionaire – was never going to work for David Gray, given Hut/Virgin/Caroline's apparent lack of interest. "There was no great love on their part and they didn't really put anything behind that record; there were a few posters went up and then they dropped me. There was no single, there was nothing. It was all a bit of a mess."

Not that this blunted his ambition or saw him stint his efforts. He pointed at bands like U2 as ones who "really came over and did America. And that's what you've got to do to get something back." The correct tactic, as he saw it, was to turn up at radio stations in Idaho, Vermont, wherever, shake the appropriate hands, do the festival the radio station puts on and build a relationship. "It's like a business. It's quite dull, in fact. But you can see how it all works, there's a vibe about it. In a country that's so big you really have to make the personal contact."

David's view of the States was laced with a healthy cynicism, as he'd tell Ireland's *Hot Press* magazine on his return. "The country is so vast and different, but to make the culture work things have been boiled down to a ludicrously simple level, with lashings of over-zealous enthusiasm. . .You go to buy a duvet and it says 'Extra Warm'. So you think that must be the warmest. But then there's like 'Extra, Extra Warm', 'Super Warm' and then, you know, 'Fucking Two Hertz, Ultra Warm, Mega Fucker That Keeps You Hot in Alaska'."

The culture shock was cushioned by the fact that David felt such an empathy with national musical icons like Hank Williams, Johnny Cash and Bruce Springsteen. Anything, in fact, with "a sort of ache at the centre of the music" that lay at the heart of Gray's own songs. And while he could scarcely be labelled a country act, the idea of Americana, alt.country or roots music was close to his heart. "When someone sings a folk song in England it seems a bit twee, because that whole thing is well and truly fucking buried," he agrees. "But here, it's a lot fresher. It's only a hundred years ago that they were killing off the last of the Indians. The blood is still on the soil, it's in people's veins, it's still a pretty wild place in many ways.

"But, as well as all that, the country is big enough to support various sub-cultures. In the UK, it's rare that you get a groovy little scene happening. But here, you can go round and sell a hundred thousand records on this slightly weird, rootsy level."

There was no doubt in David Gray's mind, if not in too many others', that he was laying the groundwork for something significant Stateside. What he didn't know was just how long it would take for the gigging and glad-handing to take off. The first breakthrough he was to enjoy was considerably closer to home, in Ireland – appropriately, given that Fishguard, not too many miles from Solva, is one of the main British ports from which ferries ply their trade to the Emerald Isle.

Nevertheless, when Gray got a phone call from someone in Dublin asking if he'd come over to play a gig, he thought they were "taking the piss". Audiences of 10 or less in England hadn't been uncommon, and, though the Shawn Colvin tour crowds had been sizeable, there was no doubting who they'd turned up to see. Why, precisely, would he have an audience in Dublin of all places?

The answer came in the shape of a man called Donal Dineen who, in 1994, had been given the task of hosting a television show called *No Disco* for the RTE channel. He'd noticed the popularity of the track 'Shine', from *Flesh*, among listeners to his *Today* FM radio show and so adopted the video for the track. He screened it regularly for the first few months of his television show in response to viewer requests, and in doing so helped it become the anthem of the year.

It had been in a packed Whelan's Pub in Dublin's Wexford Street in October 1993 that David would first encounter his Irish fan base. They in turn would discover that, if David Gray on record was beguiling, the electricity and passion he radiated in concert was a different thing entirely. That night was where David's cult following in

Ireland started, establishing a connection that would prove crucial in breaking him internationally, and lasts to this day.

Indeed, he is often considered by those who don't know him to be an Irish artist – and, given the pivotal role that country played in saving his career, it's not an impression he necessarily goes out of his way to quash. "I think that's going to be a good market for us, especially now with the situation regarding Irish artists." In echoes of Tony Cascarino, the Eire international footballer who admitted concealing his total lack of Irish ancestry from the authorities, he claims: "I am sure I have a granny somewhere!"

Even Gray can only speculate as to why he's found such favour in a country he'd barely visited before, "but from the moment I first played there the audience gave me a fantastic reaction. That was new to me. I played my own show, it was sold out the crowd went wild so I just gave it everything I kept coming back for more." The packed-house Whelan's concert turned into a tour, and the rest is history.

Looking back from the height of his fame, he mused on the Irish question. "Irish audiences are very generous, they really make an effort to make the night as special as it can be. That doesn't happen everywhere in my experience. All this success and all these marvellous nights around the country have allowed me to say yes this, *does* work I'm doing something right here I don't have to worry about it, I should just *do* it. So it's fuelled my belief in what I do."

He compared playing the same show in Sheffield on a Tuesday night "to about 40 people who don't seem to be even bothered to clap (and) at the Olympia Theatre (in Dublin). Reaction will be so different. We're not doing anything different and we always put in the effort live whether there's 50 people or whatever, so it's the punters. I don't know how it's got to the scale it has in Ireland. We didn't have a marketing budget an advertising scheme or anything we've just had word of mouth in our favour."

He was clearly upset that he remained a prophet without honour at home. "Britain's got a very blinkered kind of view of what 'groovy' stuff is – it's pretty urban and pretty 'bedsitt-y', Smithsy concept. I don't know...They've got ideas about the way it's cool to sing...You can't have a romantic, rural vision which seems to prevail in a lot of my work, and expect to gain any momentum in the system that's there – they're not interested in that; they're interested in what they think is cool, and it's not that."

Gray's visit to Belfast in early October 1994 was his fourth time in Ireland since his Whelan's debut 12 months previously, every subsequent visit to the Republic having been met with similar packed houses and a critical fervour wholly unmatched by the English press. His Galway Arts Festival show that July had seen the introduction of both a drummer and (in places) an electric guitar to his performing line-up, not to mention a swathe of new material from his second album, then but a couple of months from release. The Galway show – incidentally, his first appearance on an Irish stage with an electric guitar in his hand – would remain Gray's own most memorable performance until the Point Depot.

The Belfast appearance, at The Limelight (a venue normally reserved for mainstream indie rock), was his first in the North, and an attempt by promoters to see if 'Graymania' was a border-crossing phenomenon. Needless to say, it was. He had, however, been booked to play Belfast's Rotterdam Warehouse the previous year – but after performing 'Birds Without Wings' on TV's *Later With Jools Holland* he had apparently 'thrown a wobbler' and cancelled all his gigs until he'd got a band together. Which of course he duly had.

The estimable Neil MacColl reprised and indeed expanded on his studio role by doubling (trebling?) on electric and acoustic guitars and bass, Gray himself played both plugged and unplugged guitars while Clune (mis-credited as 'Crow', much to his amusement, in an otherwise enthusiastic Galway review) percussed as only he could. There was a lot of instrument swapping happening on stage, and a roadie had even been known to wander on with a bass in his hand by the end of the night. All this, Belfast critic Colin Harper believed, helped "temper the notion of Gray as the angry young man without much in the way of humour. The humour is there all right, but it's the power, glory, passion and metaphysical lyricism of his work that demands attention. He may not be the type of chap one could easily relate to socially, but on a purely artistic level he is, for what this opinion may be worth, an exceptional talent."

High praise indeed. But David Gray would discover a down side to all this Emerald excess. "We used to try to get record people to come over to see, you've got to come to see it in Dublin. There's be a fantastic gig, great atmosphere, packed out and everything. Then they'd say but it's different over here. You'd think how are Irish people profoundly different? Are English people incapable of enjoying our music? That was obviously just complete rubbish.

"Because we have been discovered in Ireland it doesn't really endear us to fashion conscious-British music press. We just have to stick to what we are good at, playing music, keep the gigs doing well and keep making good records and I know we will get there eventually. If the truth be told we have neglected the UK for the past four years, so there is a lot of catching up to be done."

His Irish success would spawn not only a nation of 'Grayites' but a bunch of copycat singer-songwriters "It's a compliment, isn't it?," remarked the original. "After all the years that I wanted to be like other people, it's weird to think that someone wants to be like me. You see people on stage and you think they're amazing but you never imagine that someone is thinking that about you. It's weird, man!"

Even more Grayites were over-zealous fans, for whom David felt a certain amount of concern. "They're so impressionable, they take it all so incredibly seriously. . . but sometimes it just goes a bit too far." He concluded that it was his own fault. "I listen to the lunatic screaming on my own records. . . they were bound to come out of the woodwork, as if I'd written 'Follow me!' backwards between the grooves of the record."

Gray was becoming suspicious of "loaded questions about how important Ireland is to me and how much I care about the place. I haven't quite worked it all out and I don't want to over-think it. I don't dwell on it too much." According to his champion Donal Dineen – a man some have said is the Paolo Hewitt to Gray's Paul Weller – there was no secret why Ireland had taken him to their collective bosom. Gray "comes down in a line from all the best stuff, all the way through Van Morrison, Bob Dylan, all the best songwriters – that's the class he's in. The thing about him, that he's not successful worldwide, is that he's definitely out of time. I think he's ahead of it."

The song 'Shine' would become a classic encore number (often laughingly and confusingly dedicated to "the two people who bought my first record") and receive the seal of approval when Irish first lady of song Mary Black titled her 1997 album after it. This would be released on the Dara label (Curb in the US), and is required listening for any David Gray fan. He didn't actually play on the album, which was produced by Joni Mitchell's bass-playing ex-husband Larry Klein, but no fewer than five of his songs were featured alongside material from such respected writers as Richard Thompson and Paul Brady.

Two of the songs, 'Shine' and 'Late Night Radio', would also be recorded and released by their writer – but 'Almost Gone', 'Trespass Shoes' and 'What Does It Matter' appear to have been donated solely and specifically to Ms Black. (Indeed, 'Trespass Shoes' appeared to have been written from a female perspective.) David featured third in a 'thanks' list headed by Paul Brady and Ray Davies, though where the Kinks songwriter (if indeed it was he) fitted in was unclear since none of his songs were included.

Black had made her name in the Eighties as lead singer with well-known folk group De Dannan, and her music was especially popular with the expatriate community in the United States – hence 'Shine' being recorded at the famed Capitol Studios in Hollywood. And it's quite possible that Black's firm friendship with Joan Baez, with whom she'd performed and recorded, was what led to the latter's previously mentioned Dylan comparison.

As an afterthought, *A Century Ends* producer Dave Anderson remembers "going to Windmill Lane studios in Dublin, when I was working with a band called Superstar, years after the album had come out. I walked onto the control room and there was a copy of *A Century Ends* lying on the mixing desk. I asked the assistant engineer what it was doing there and he said 'Didn't you know? It's big in Ireland'."

Amidst his current loved-up bliss, David had been hit by a domestic crisis when his parents split just four months after his own marriage. "It's suddenly very odd," he told Q magazine, "to consider your parents who are your parents rather than being two people, being out in the world, getting off with people. Their vulnerability is suddenly incredibly obvious." It understandably affected him deeply. "The idea of home was obliterated, there was nowhere to go for Christmas. I had to re-evaluate everything, what was real and what wasn't because I never noticed any problems."

And another divorce, between Gray and Hut Records, would soon throw his life into even more disarray. . .

CHAPTER 4

Sell, Sell, Sellout

David was fortunate indeed, or so it seemed, that the moment Virgin dropped him EMI were waiting in the wings to pick him up. "I think it was January the second (1995), the first day they could drop me they dropped me, and then next day the phone rang. It was EMI in America saying we had a bit of a fan there, this Brian Koppelman fella, saying, 'I'm gonna fly over in the private jet, I wanna meet Dave and offer you a record deal. What do you want, come and work with me, I think you could be big in America.' It was music to our ears."

The whole process was an eye-opener for David Gray as he'd always assumed that, once you lost your record deal, that was the end of your career. "What a complete lie *that* was. Look at the charts and you'll see everyone's been around seven or eight times." Interestingly, A&R guru Koppelman had been impressed not by the most recent *Flesh* but *A Century Ends*.

Funnily enough, that was how David himself had felt when talking to Colin Harper the previous October "You've got to keep working, got to keep moving. I'll hopefully be doing another album soon." To underline how much of a commercial dead duck Gray was in his home country, Harper had been hawking his interview of the

51

previous October to every reputable music magazine around – with almost totally negative results. "It was a time when virtually every editor I was dealing with turned down a Gray feature – except Ian Anderson at *Folk Roots*. He was prepared to give the benefit of the doubt to a writer's enthusiasms, and I think that enlightenment should be recognised!"

Harper felt Gray "wasn't a natural to the business of 'being in the music business.' " "He disliked interviews, was bored by the long hours of travelling, frustrated by the long haul of 'cracking' England and ridden with angst at the indifference and ill-informed opinions he'd experienced in parts of the media. But such is the down-side of genius. . ."

In that interview, Gray had also almost predicted his own falling-out with Hut months before it actually came to pass. "Nothing surprises me about what the music business will do for a cheap trick," he told Harper. "It's a sad fucking industry. It works the same as any industry and that's why it's sad – because it's dealing with something precious. You can see why forces prevail – it's about money basically. Unfortunately there's quite a fragile human process right at the root of it, which is making music, which can be easily destroyed by its rather heavy-handed techniques. So we'll just have to hope that more and more things get enough space to grow.

"The industry doesn't seem willing to work things through. They say they're interested in long term acts but they're not interested in anything that subverts their sales ideas. They want formulas that work. Singing songs is always gonna be valuable to humankind – always has been. It's about words and the simplest arrangements of music; it'll always be valuable. It's not going to fade away. They seem to have a problem with investment – to go against the grain and let something grow on its own merits. Because someone invented hype, it's like all you have to do is hit this fantastic button and someone starts selling loads of records.

"Everyone wants to use that technique now, and it's like 'Why not?' – when you're selling what is just musical product, why not hit the hype button every time and if you get it right you sell millions, and who cares if they're burnt out in a couple of years, 'cos you'll just hit it again with somebody else. So there's this fast turnover of what are people. It's a depressing trend, that things seem to get chewed up and spat out pretty quickly."

One band which had lately struggled through the vicissitudes of the music machine to come up trumps were Radiohead – and when the chance came up to accompany them on a six-week tour of the States in May and June, the fact he had yet to open his account for his new label did not bother David Gray one jot.

The Oxford five-piece were, at that point, a totally hot band in US sales terms. After several years in the wilderness, they were finally tasting the first fruits of fame and fortune thanks to their single 'Creep' suddenly going ballistic, courtesy of US college radio and MTV. The next step was to not only maintain that unexpected level of success but to expand on it.

Having played a stop-start world trek over the previous 12 months, they now made the States a priority as their second album *The Bends* was prepared for release. They travelled to Boston in May to start another US tour that was set to close at the Palace, Los Angeles on 15 June. And David Gray was along for the ride. The line-up was a basic three piece of Clune, David and David Nolté, previous tours having also featured Neill MacColl on guitar.

The Radiohead connection came about because the band's Thom Yorke and Jonny Greenwood were fans of the first album, *A Century Ends*. Hearing this, David's manager suggested he open for them in America. "It was weird," Gray later recounted. "We got on like a house on fire. It was an unlikely combination but it worked. That was a great tour." He's since affectionately accused Yorke of stealing his manic head movements. . .

Legend has it that, on one occasion during the tour, David and his band set fire to the headliners' dressing room. This appears to have been an elaboration of the truth, and that David had actually strewn empty crisp packets on the floor of the backstage area to make it easier for him to accomplish an impression of Michael Jackson doing his celebrated Moonwalk. The blame was put fairly and squarely on the expedition's drink of choice – the Sea Breeze, a healthy mixture of vodka, grapefruit and cranberry juice – and Radiohead were understanding to the point that they even cleaned up afterwards!

David was certainly awe-struck on the nights he watched from the wings rather than attempting Jacko's dance stunts. "Radiohead were really taking off," he marvelled, "and I certainly learned a thing or two about professionalism from them. They really do it, those boys, they really deliver night after night – what a brilliant band to watch up close."

In 2001, he would return to the relationship with a suggestion that he'd like to try a joint musical venture at some point. "The only person (sic) that I've met that tickled my fancy was Radiohead, I made friends with them on tour and they're both incredibly gifted and I had a little jam with Thom (Yorke) one night. He blew me away, the way he thinks about music; collaborating with him would be great."

Faced with opening for such a dynamic act, Gray and his musicians formulated an 'up and at 'em' strategy, hitting hard from the first whistle and receiving approval from audiences who frankly didn't have the first idea of who they were or where they came from. "If you do anything with enough gusto, people will just get into it," he confirmed, adding "We're not like shrinking violets on the stage."

He was under no illusions as to the long-term nature of the job he faced. "You've really got to *do* it. I think that's why not many British bands have been cracking America. They get success over there and they think that all they have to bring to America is their cool. They turn up in New York, LA, San Francisco, do a few shows and fuck off again, and think the whole thing is going to fall into place. Like, go on record company, weave your magic."

A second Radiohead tour in 1996 would result from ill health befalling Sparklehorse frontman Mark Linkous. He'd come to Europe to support the band, but accidentally overdosed on a cocktail of prescription anti-depressants, Valium and alcohol. Unconscious for 14 hours in his hotel room, he suffered a heart attack and nerve damage which would keep him wheelchair-bound for a year.

Radiohead and the Gray trio happily reconvened their partnership, albeit in the saddest of circumstances, with the support act's tour bus "debauched idiocy" compared with the more businesslike headliners' vehicle. "One night they stayed over like a pyjama party, and we played them Captain Beefheart's *Clear Spot* again and again. This record blew us all away, and there's a track on their new record ('Amnesiac') that sounds like it... is that down to me?"

The big influence in David Gray's music at this time was not Captain Beefheart, nor even Dylan, Waits or Morrison, but a more unpredicted and unpredictable figure – Kurt Cobain, leader of Seattle rockers Nirvana and figurehead of the grunge generation. They're still a personal favourite of his, but in this case, "I persuaded myself that perhaps the rockier side of things was worth pursuing." Cobain had blown his brains out in April 1994, ensuring himself the ever-youthful immortality of a James Dean, Marc Bolan or Sid Vicious.

New paymasters EMI were now calling the shots and suggested Gray record the new album in the States with Grant Lee Buffalo bass player and pianist Paul Kimble at the production helm. Alongside singer-guitarist Grant Lee Phillips, Kimble had been the driving force behind a band whose 1993 début *Fuzzy* had been lauded in print by R.E.M.'s Michael Stipe as his pick of the year. His production of follow-ups *Mighty Joe Moon* (1994) and *Copperopolis* (1995) had established Phillips as a rising star, the variety of instruments used to create the music, from pedal steel to pump organ, particularly notable.

When Colin Harper asked Gray in December 1994 if there was "anyone he admired on the songwriting front who's relatively new?", cunningly avoiding the well-worn Dylan/Waits/Morrison furrow, David had nominated Grant Lee Buffalo. They seem to be doing something pretty worthwhile. He's obviously worked a few things out. Their second record was a real development from the first one – good stuff."

Accordingly, Gray and Clune flew out to meet both the US-based Nolté and the Buffalo mainman at his Ithaca, New York State stronghold. Unfortunately the arranged marriage quickly soured and, after three weeks of painstaking instrumental work in which Gray claims he had yet to lay down a single vocal track, the patience of a man who'd admitted just months earlier that "after a couple of hours in the studio I'm gone" finally snapped.

"He never wanted us to be there," Gray claimed. "Eventually I just stormed in and said 'Fuck this, we're going to do it how we want'. He was going to have to get paid, but we went back to England and tried to fix the record up ourselves." So much for the "incredible record" they'd travelled out in the expectation of making!

David Nolté tells a similar story, if in more restrained fashion. "We spent six weeks recording and mixing and the end result was not what we were looking for. Dave, Clune and I had become a team by this time, we had a few tours under our belts and had developed the material together during these tours. We couldn't seem to get the sounds or performances we needed with Paul. He had a very different way of working and it all ended badly."

At this point, happy to report, fortune and fate took a hand. Prior to recording with Kimble, Nolté had done 8-track demos of the songs in his native Los Angeles, where he had "produced a lot of stuff prior to this, but you would have never heard of any of the bands. Dave really liked what I had done so, when the Paul Kimble recordings didn't work out, he convinced the record company to let me have a go."

As with *Flesh*, though, the result would be a compromise, the record company insisting on some of the earlier work they'd paid for surviving to form part of the final release. This resulted in the finished article bearing a tortuous trail of production and recording credits. The album was 'Produced by David Nolté, mixed by Bob Salcedo and David Nolté and recorded by Paul Kimble and Brian Zee at Pyramid Sound, Ithaca'. That complex caveat only applied to half the 12 tracks, however. Of the remainder, three were cut in Air London, one across the capital at Pink Floyd's Britannia Row studios and two more in Los Angeles.

Bob Salcedo was an engineer David Nolté had worked with in LA. "I thought he would do a good job, so I brought him with me to England to do the record. He worked on Madonna's *Like A Prayer* album and some Sheryl Crow stuff as well as a ton of other things. He had similar sensibilities when it came to compression, reverb and EQ, and those were some of the biggest problems with the Paul Kimble tapes."

From its very title onwards, *Sell, Sell, Sell* had a confrontational edge. Gray stared myopically out from the cover of his first release in nearly two years, the left lens of his glasses obscured by price stickers.

These bore a number which could have been 999 – the British emergency telephone code – or 666, the Number of the Beast familiar to all fully paid-up Iron Maiden fans. In view of the circumstances either could, conceivably, have been relevant.

Five years later, David Nolté was still giving little away. "The significance of the weird cover art? It was the image that made it okay to name the album *Sell, Sell, Sell*. I thought it summed it all up perfectly!"

The full-sounding release had the air of a collaboration, a band effort rather than a solo record. It was certainly more upbeat than either *A Century Ends* or *Flesh*, definitely, defiantly 'plugged' rather than acoustic, and held together pretty well given the trying circumstances of its piecemeal creation in various corners of the globe. David Nolté appeared to be the glue that had held it all together, being credited as producer as well as contributing 'bass, lead guitars, piano, organ, etc, etc'. "I played most of the electric guitar... Dave plays electric rhythm on a couple of tracks." The faithful Clune (who'd add bass to 'Hold On To Nothing') offered drums and backing vocals throughout.

As for that title, Gray confessed to some cynicism creeping through – not to mention a mischievous desire to see what his new label would make of the whole thing. "It's a line in one of the songs: 'Praise the Lord above and sell, sell, sell'. Perhaps the most cynical line on the record. I don't know why I was tempted to use it as a title. I think I liked it because it was simple. Possibly half my mind was thinking, 'Well, we'll see what EMI does with this'. It's the third time I've had a major record deal so I was wary about how they were going to deal with it after all the big claims of how successful they would make it, et cetera."

Late, great soul superstar Marvin Gaye had famously created an album, *There My Dear*, in 1978 to fulfil his financial obligations when he divorced his employer, Motown Records boss Berry Gordy's daughter. But for David Gray, a key event in his recent life mirrored in *Sell, Sell, Sell* was his parents' divorce. Reflections included the wedding-dress mannequin on the back cover, and a single word, 'Divorced?', picked out in lights as if on a noticeboard.

Musically, the questioning lyric of 'Gutters Full Of Rain' dealt candidly with the subject. He admitted "the emotions I felt surfaced as a current in some of the songs that are on the record." The break-up, he confessed, had "absolutely altered my relationship with them, it has had a profound effect. It has made everything completely different, my whole slant on the past, and the way things actually were, and what I actually saw, and what I didn't see. My whole take on the family unit has been shattered by what's happened, and the things I have found out since then have had a massive effect on my relationship in the family and on myself."

The album opened stridently enough with 'Faster, Sooner, Now', where he was already stressing "there's nowhere I belong". The distinction between acoustic (Gray) and electric (Nolté) guitars was fairly clear, David offering an attractively droned strum. Track two, 'Late Night Radio', would be the song for which this album would be remembered – its quasi-single status relying on a US promotional release and a video which has since received far more airings than it did at the time. It was one of two tracks to survive from the Paul Kimble sessions, though it had undergone two more spells of 'additional recording'

Next up was the title track, the verses stark, the choruses drenched in electric guitar and an horrendous rock guitar break in the middle. By total contrast, 'Hold On To Nothing' could well have come from one of the first two albums in its stark simplicity, Clune adding a subtle bass to proceedings. 'Everytime', too, boasted the hypnotic repetition that has become a David Gray trademark, though this time in a band setting with electric guitar mercifully absent. Hue and Cry singer turned broadsheet rock critic Pat Kane later highlighted this song as typical of "a kind of subterranean, very homesick bluesiness" David had left behind him en route to attracting a mass audience with *White Ladder*. "Gray spits out more ornate metaphors in one song ('Your spine a white ladder, your eyes singing sadder. . . nightingales calling, shooting stars falling. . .') than in the rest of the new album put together. As it was recorded in LA, for an American record company which wasn't giving a cold taco at the time, you can understand the overreaching."

'Magdelena' sounds a suspiciously Morrison-esque song title and there's a touch of 'Brown-Eyed Girl' in its acoustic lope – not to mention a vocal 'na-na-na' section. It's also the second song in a row to boast a London reference.

'Smile' returned us to the solo Gray of yesteryear, suggesting a song he'd had in his locker for a while. The observational touches, the "sunrise turning the teradrops gold" marked this one down as a keeper. Next came the other Paul Kimble track to survive: 'Only The Lonely', no relation to the Roy Orbison classic, was a strummy, American-sounding number.

'What Am I Doing Wrong?' keeps the listener waiting for Gray's entrance, but the song – 'What am I doing wrong/you don't telephone' – isn't really worth the wait. Unlike 'Gutters Full Of Rain', the previously mentioned ballad encapsulating his feelings on his parents' break-up. 'The thief who stole my life/Has taken too my faith/I can see now how the world gets twisted."

Like 'Gutters. . .', the last two songs, 'Forever Is Tomorrow Is Today' and 'Folk Song', were recorded in London after the rest of the album. 'Forever. . .' dismisses a hedonistic lifestyle with 'We're gonna need more than money and science/to see us through this world.' Even when the drums and bass weigh in, 'Folk Song' ends an album that emerged despite the problems that had beset its recording, and sometimes it sounds like it. There's a touch of 'It's All Over' as he bemoans a promise of marriage that failed to materialise. 'There's no light in heaven/that can shine for me' he howls over a funereal piano.

Despite the optimistic title, it would be his next album, not *Sell, Sell, Sell*, that would finally break David Gray commercially and garner a massive international audience. Still, *Sell, Sell, Sell* did receive critical acclaim and found fans in Dave Matthews and Radiohead, both acts with which he would/had toured. Musically, Gray had approached his third album with a more mainstream sensibility, largely eschewing the sparseness of his earlier recordings for a more intricate sound. The result was his poppiest recording to date and one which seemed at least vaguely in tune with the American airwaves.

David Nolté, the man who'd carried the burden of delivering Gray's 'baby', freely admits that by the time the record was finished, "I had no real perspective left. I thought we'd done a good job and the record company seemed happy, but it hadn't been as organic and effortless as it should have been. In retrospect, we should have taken a couple of months to rethink everything and then started fresh. We ended up trying to fix the tracks that Paul had started and that was a mistake.

"Songs I'm proud of for different reasons," he concluded, "are 'Late Night Radio', 'Everytime', 'Hold On To Nothing' and 'Smile'. They're all good but yeah, I would do everything differently if I could."

For Gray himself, also in retrospect, the decision to swathe his music in electric guitars had simply not come off. "I knew absolutely that it wasn't worth doing because it didn't suit my style," he told *Guitar World Acoustic* magazine some time later. "All the best things on the record, just about, were the more intimate moments. That's where my strength lies. Also, I was frustrated with the sort of standard band set-up. We'd given it a go, and there were other people who were doing it so much better. With two electric guitars thrashing away, you don't get as close to the songs."

EMI's Koppelman, the man who'd 'rediscovered' Gray, had a campaign plan to follow up the US release of *Sell, Sell, Sell* with some heavy touring. "We talked about what we wanted," David explains, "and he said what he was going to do. We're gonna send you out on the road, you can play your own shows, build a fan base. It made a lot of sense but just evaporated, unfortunately. You could see it. You'd do an interview with someone who hadn't even heard of you, they were reading your biography they'd just that moment been given. You can see the whole thing just wasn't working."

The American reaction to his music on a fan rather than a critical level differed widely. "Some of them seem to go wild for it, in other places they just sit there like they've had a frontal lobotomy and just can't wait to go down to McDonald's."

The main problem, as the singer saw it, was aiming the music at the wrong place. He summed up his record company's philosophy thus: "We're going to take the Midwest, send you in there and if you can crack the Midwest we'll take it to the whole county. But why the Midwest, for Christ's sake? We had no following there. New York, maybe. In New York we had a following. They sent us to these miserable shitholes in the Midwest."

This led to the tale of being second-billed in Rock Island, Illinois, to the latest culinary attraction, an anecdote Gray has trotted out more than a few times. *Hot Press* was one of the first recipients. "They sent us out on some fucking bullshit, half-assed scheme," he told them. "It was really depressing. We arrived at one venue and there was a huge sign outside: 'Tonight: Barbecue Ribs – Sold Out. (next line) David Gray – 8 o'clock.' When you're less of a draw than barbecue ribs, you've got to ask yourself some serious questions!"

It got worse. The following night, in Toledo, the band peered out through the backstage drapes to find their support act playing to around 250 people. "We thought, 'fuck, this is cool'. Then a door at the back of the room opened and everyone went down to a club. We played to about eight people, while this throbbing kind of country techno club was packed by freakish people with eyes on the wrong side of their face and hairy teeth! It was like being inside a Hieronymus Bosch painting."

The tour after *Sell, Sell, Sell* was released found David Nolté switching from bass to lead guitar, the omnipresent Clune behind the kit as ever. Bass and backing vocal duties were assumed by the previously mentioned Kristi Callan, on whose identity David Nolté will elaborate. "Kristi is from other bands I had played with…in the mid-Eighties I joined her band Wednesday Week who were signed to Enigma Records and put out one album called *What We Had*. Kristi and I have been married for over eight years (in 2001) and have two young children."

With their new record company reluctant to shell out too much money on an untried talent, Gray and chums were operating on a tight budget. So much so that, instead of paying for hotel rooms, they decided to opt for a second-hand sleeper bus and use it as a movable base. This set up a bizarre tale in which they found themselves abandoned out on the interstate by a lovesick driver.

"We basically got the crappiest sleeper bus in the US; this thing had done nearly two million miles in 20 years going around and around America. The driver had been in it the whole time, a sort of Hobbit type with really long hair; we should have known there was something really funny about him. He had contact lenses and he never took them out, just squirted stuff in them early in the morning. This guy lost his mind on the tour. He fell in love with a woman and asked us if she could come on the bus for the rest of the tour, and I said, 'absolutely not!'."

The spurned driver decided to take matters into his own hands and faked the bus breaking down "in the middle of nowhere, in the middle of winter. It was in a place like Hicksville. We pulled into some garage and he said, 'There's something wrong with my back tyre, we'll have to pull in here'. And it was a little café with one guy behind the counter, with teeth going everywhere. This guy in the bus had tampered with the electrics so all the power went off.

"We were watching the video in the bus and we all had to go into the café and the moment we'd got into the café, he proceeded to drive off into the distance. He took all our gear, everything. . . back towards Seattle. We were left open-mouthed."

Gray called the police, who chased the errant bus for over a hundred miles before catching up with it. When they caught the driver they couldn't do anything about it because it was a civil matter – and three gigs went west as a result.

It was hardly surprising that tour madness started to set in, and in a big way. "People started going insane. It did get depressing and it was a real trial. I talked to Clune and we'd go, 'Jesus this isn't right, record company bastards'. You get very cynical and it becomes us and them which is real bullshit because they're just people doing their jobs at the end of the day in a dysfunctional environment."

What was in fact happening behind the scenes was that EMI America, the company he had rushed into bed with, was on the point of going out of business. Understandably, company employees were worried about their own futures, and unproven talent like David Gray was very much at the bottom of everyone's 'To Do' lists. A few promo one-track singles were released – 'Faster Sooner Now' and 'Late Night Radio' were both apparently serviced to US radio during David's tour with Radiohead, but barely reached an audience. Promotion was minimal, and the album's sales inevitably suffered. First time out, *Sell, Sell, Sell* is said to have sold, sold, sold less than 5,000 copies.

Even worse was that Europe, his most successful market to date, had been last to hear his latest release. Little wonder that, immediately before EMI America's final collapse, Gray sent his lawyers in to buy out his contract. He wasn't concerned with royalties, just "get me out of this damn mess!" By this time the singer had endured so much humiliation he'd almost begun to enjoy it. "I was marinated in failure," he now says. "I'd just sort of take it all on the chin. When something bad would happen, I'd laugh, like, 'Bring it on. I've seen much worse.'"

Bruised but unbowed by "our disastrous summer tour", Gray headed back across the Atlantic and spent the next few months at home in London – "brooding, drinking a lot." With two record deals having gone awry, little wonder "Fucked off" was the expression he used to describe how he felt about the business side of things. He also parted company with the music publishing firm, Warner Chappell, with whom he'd been linked since before Hut Records days. They'd shown faith in him when record labels had not, but had finally been forced to cut loose a man whose potential had yet to be translated into earnings. He still had the Martin guitar he'd bought with his first advance, but this latest rejection at the hands of the music business only served to magnify the feelings of desperation.

He even briefly considered becoming a milkman. But, having touched bottom, he was determined to swim, not sink. "Part of me was determined not to dwell on the negative side of it like the record companies, the commercial failures and the business not happening. "I'd rather just be making the music that I find uplifting. I wanted to concentrate on the good things that do happen, 'cos otherwise I'd have end up a miserable old wreck. You find so many people in bars grumbling on about the music business and what should have happened. I was determined not to be a martyr to that cause."

The experienced Rob Holden realised they now faced an uphill battle. "David had already had record deals in England and America, and as far as the industry was concerned, he was bad meat. Nobody was going to go out of their way to help us any more."

Faced with this situation, David reacted in what he'd later admit was a less that constructive manner by, firstly, splitting from his manager and secondly overdoing the drink and drugs to an extent that he risked splitting with his life partner Olivia too. "It took a while to shake off the negativity," he now says. "I needed to know, at a nuts and bolts level, why I was doing this. Giving up entered my mind, but it didn't stay there."

63

Regarding long-time mentor Holden, he "didn't want to receive his wisdom, the bigger picture" – but he certainly didn't dispense with him as a friend. "Occasionally I'd end up back at Rob's (after) sticking things up my nose," he told Q magazine in October 2000 (the 'chemicals rushing through my bloodstream' reference in 'Babylon' inevitably comes to mind here.) He doesn't recommend cocaine, however, explaining that it increases your ability to drink alcohol to the point that "you completely and utterly poison yourself, to the point that you think you're going to die. It's not a hangover any more, you're hanging on for dear life."

Holden for his part understood why his services had been dispensed with. "I was gutted," he told *Top* magazine, "but with hindsight it was probably right. You do tend to blame each other when things aren't going right, and we needed head space." Gray: "After all the disasters, I didn't want to hear anybody's else's wisdom about how it should be," he says. "Once I understood what I felt, I approached some other managers, but it felt really weird. It was like 'Fucking hell, Rob! Let me back!'"

In an effort to analyse what had gone wrong every bad review was re-read, every slating suffered a second time. "You look at yourself and you think you've done something wrong and look at everyone else and think they're doing something wrong. It's painful You're putting your heart out and it seems to be being ignored, almost ridiculed at times.

"I got slated in a few papers and you just think am I slow on the uptake here, maybe I shouldn't be doing this. It just isn't working out, But eventually I calmed down and said yes, I still feel good about the music, I have something to offer. I had to open myself up, give more away, open my heart up to the whole thing again."

Holden's faith in his charge commendably never wavered. "I felt very passionately about it, and I thought 'Well if I'm wrong about this, I'm wrong about everything'. What was remarkable was the way that we kept reinventing David's career in our heads. Whether that was commendable or it should have been treated medically is another matter!"

With no income to speak of coming in, Olivia Gray became the family breadwinner. She had just started her career as a lawyer and was able to keep up the mortgage payments when David's income dwindled to nothing. "These events have become so mythologised," Gray would later smile. "But I'm always wary of calling them 'hard times,' because, fuck me, they're not hard times. Let's go have a walk around the streets and see some people having some hard times. I had a terraced house in Stoke Newington. I had a wife, and a career, even if it was going nowhere."

Having been told to sort himself out – on several occasions – by his nearest and dearest, he gave up "rolling in at ten in the morning having gone out and got completely and utterly fucked up" and resolved to turn his confusion into songs. "I looked at all the work I'd done and how badly it had all gone, and I thought, 'Can I do better?'"

The result would be *White Ladder*.

CHAPTER 5

Creating *White Ladder*

The success of *White Ladder* proves that miracles do happen. But it was a question of being in the right place at the right time. Unknown to David Gray, the trend towards more sensitive music that would see the likes of Travis and Coldplay in the Top 10 was on the horizon: in one pundit's phrase, the perception "quiet is the new loud" was about to gain currency.

The integration of left-field bands into the musical mainstream, a process that arguably started with the Blur-Oasis Brit-pop chart wars in 1995, was moving on apace. It would make household names of the likes of Radiohead, but claim the occasional casualty – like *Select* magazine, slogan 'Music For Tomorrow', which found that after a decade of existence it no longer had an exclusive constituency.

The need to be in the right place at the right time could not have been illustrated more cogently than by The Fat Lady Sings, a Dublin band whose 1986–1994 career had both overlapped and interlinked with David Gray's. Not only that, but lead vocalist/songwriter Nick Kelly was a figure not dissimilar to Gray whose impassioned vocals had been likened to the Beautiful South's Paul Heaton. The band – Kelly, Dermot Lynch (bass and keyboards), Rob Hamilton (drums) and Tim Bradshaw (guitar) – eerily predicted David Gray's move from indie to East West by following four independent singles with two albums on the major label; the occasional song title like 'Drunkard Logic' also had a Gray-like resonance.

Kelly quit, disillusioned, after a US tour in 1993 that had been tipped to shoot them into the big league – and his account of the experience that tipped him over the edge sounds remarkably like Gray's darkest hour. It happened at a ballroom in Baltimore where TFLS were sharing the bill with three other bands. "The only people in the audience were the members of the other three bands, who were waiting for us to finish, so that they could play their set to us." Kelly wanted out, and got his wish in January the following year. "I don't want to do this anymore," he said. "I don't want to spend nine months a year in a bus and I don't want to have to sit all my life in meetings, talking about whether (or not) I can write songs."

In echoes of David Gray's first three unprofitable albums, The Fat Lady Sings managed to amass total debts of £600,000 before splitting, despite selling a respectable 40,000 copies of each of their albums.* Kelly had retired to a day job in advertising, but released the solo *Between Trapezes* on his own label and sold 5,000 straight off the bat. "No major label could make a profit on that, but I make a good profit," he explained.

Kelly's hymn to freedom from the shackles of the record business must have been music to David Gray's ears as he set out to create a career-changing album on next to no money. "I'm a one-man operation," Kelly proudly stated. "I really do feel that I have a little corner shop to myself and I'm nice to the customers – I'm delighted when they buy my cheese. I didn't like being a wage slave. Not having a huge amount of people around me also makes a big difference – band, management, record company etc are always on tenterhooks for you to be successful. And with the best will in the world, they can't help putting pressure on you. All of that is now gone."

So how do we know David Gray followed the fortunes of The Fat Lady Sings? We know because he had co-opted Dermot Lynch and Tim Bradshaw as supporting musicians in 1996, just as they were

* An industry source has speculated David's trio sold marginally half that in total their first time round.

enjoying success with their next band, formed with songwriter and former TFLS support act Peter Stewart. 'Everything Falls Apart', a track from the first album, had given Dog's Eye View (as they christened themselves) an immediate US hit single, but any amount of follow-ups failed. Sadly for Lynch and Bradshaw, that coincided with Gray's own retrenchment. "We were playing with David at the same time," Dermot Lynch recalls, "but then he went into a bit of a slow period and we had to look for other things." It would not, however, be the last time Tim Bradshaw's name cropped up in the David Gray story.

The musical elements Gray was bringing to the recording of the new album echoed some of his favourite albums by others. Bob Dylan's *Bringing It All Back Home*, for instance, the 1965 recording containing the seminal 'Mr Tambourine Man' where his hero. . . "knocked the folk thing on the head for good. It's spiky, like barbed wire. His vocals were done in a couple of takes: Dylan definitely was not into polishing things. This was an instinctive record. He was moving so fast, he didn't have time to mess about." That first-take attitude would be evident throughout *White Ladder*.

The electronic experimentation David was bringing to bear may have had something to do with the album by French electro-poppers Air he was listening to, but he also deferred to John Martyn, the folkie with an Echoplex whose sonic innovations in the Seventies were later echoed by the likes of Beth Orton. "He's continually trying to push the boat out, perhaps because he hasn't ever really had the success. He's always looking to unlock the door and move his music on." A spirit of experimentation, letting the effects direct the music as much as modifying the sound, would rule.

He was also warming to the rough and ready, no rules approach of Captain Beefheart – who, with his famed Magic Band, produced some of the most way-out music of the Sixties and Seventies. "He's not really everybody's cup of tea [but] he just proves that if you write music, you can do anything you like. The rules are set by you to make you feel comfortable. You paint your own boundaries. But Beefheart constantly went out there." The word paint may have some importance there: like David, the former Don Van Vliet was a keen painter, and indeed had retired to a trailer park in the Mojave desert with his wife Jan to concentrate on his art.

Gray had then re-evaluated John Lennon's work, having listened back to it while trying to think of a cover version to do. "When you listen back to this, it's staggering how rough his recordings were," said a man who was barely out of short trousers when the ex-Beatle was gunned down in 1980. His selection for a possible cover had been 'Jealous Guy', a track from the *Imagine* album. "I was amazed at how shoddy it was, but still great. There's such a hunger in the voice; it's the same with Van Morrison. They need the music so badly, they pursue it [and] it's like a torch burning for them."

All these musical ingredients and more were being marshalled to make a dramatic right-angled turn from the well-worn singer-songwriter highway. But with resources at a premium, *White Ladder* owed its very creation to Gray being asked to contribute no fewer than five songs to a new film.* "We got a lucky break with this feature film being made in England by this Scottish director," he'd later explain. "The director asked me to do the theme music, and that came in at just the right moment. We didn't get very much money, but all of it went into the record. And we went around begging people in the industry who were fans and said, 'Can you chip in?' So we just begged, borrowed, stole, and everything else, and that's how we got it together."

This Year's Love tells the story of six young people all mixing in intersecting social circles in the north London district of Camden Town, an area one critic termed "a trendy inner-city London enclave with its street markets and music venues, moneyed chic and artistic poverty, ethnic restaurants and canals." The film's (American-born) producer, Michele Camarda, was keen to feature "some of the best clubs and hippest bands in London", likening Camden to New York's Greenwich Village and Soho, while writer/director David Kane thought "the fact that all the characters live there makes all the coincidences more believable."

It starts dramatically at the wedding of flighty Hannah (played by Catherine McCormack) and volatile Scot Danny (Douglas Henshall). Their marriage is destined to last just 37 minutes, Danny's

---

* David and Clune would also appear as the resident band of the pub in which the film's characters drank.

discovery that Hannah slept with his best man the week before the wedding leading to wedding-cake throwing and a dramatic walk-outs. Everything that follows owes something to this cataclysmic event.

Best-known name among the cast was Kathy Burke, acclaimed for her role as the abused wife in Gary Oldman's *Nil By Mouth* and, more recently, TV funnyman Harry Enfield's teenage sidekick Perry. She played Marey, who worked as a cleaner at Heathrow airport and met Danny when he turned up at Terminal Four and offered her his spare ticket to Jamaica, his honeymoon destination. But he's too drunk to be allowed on the plane, so they end up rolling off together and eventually cohabiting.

This was a repeating theme of the film, each of the three male and three female characters falling in and out of bed with each other before the unhappily married couple eventually settle their differences and return to Heathrow en route for a delayed honeymoon. The theory was that only on your eighth relationship will you find a satisfactory partner. . . the trick is obviously staying sober enough to keep count.

Dreadlocked single mother and ex-public schoolgirl Sophie was played by Jennifer Ehle, of *Pride And Prejudice* fame – though she had gained rock'n'roll credentials by playing John Lennon's wife, Cynthia in *Backbeat*. Her character had an improbable liaison with Elvis Costello lookalike Liam (Ian Hart), while long-haired lothario Cameron (Dougray Scott) and Alice (Emily Woof, who'd played opposite Ewan McGregor in flop glam-rock movie *Velvet Goldmine*) made up the numbers in a curious mating/dating game.

Musical director of the project was Simon Boswell, who'd found brief fame with Seventies power poppers Advertising before moving into television and films. Given David Gray's involvement in the fabric of the film, it was surprising that the Stereophonics' 'Just Looking' should have been chosen as the opening title theme, but the Welsh band were certainly on the higher steps of the fame escalator at the point of release. Other, hipper contributors to the soundtrack, albeit with 'off-the-shelf' offerings, included Travis, BMX Bandits, Ocean Colour Scene, The La's and Garbage.

But none of these famous names could claim to have appeared in the film itself. The connection came thanks to airport cleaner Marey singing in a pub, the Three Fiddlers, with a band who just happened to feature David and Clune! The numbers were made up by an (actor) bass player, Burke adding backing vocals, tambourine and (on 'Sail Away') barely audible keyboard.

Five of David's numbers were featured in the show'; curiously, 'This Year's Love' itself was the least obvious in its brief appearance as background music. Its companion on the film soundtrack, released by V2 Records, was 'Monday Morning', a mid-paced number as unremarkable as the Fleetwood Mac song with which it shared its title. David craves nicotine, complains he can't make it on his own and generally bemoans his lot in a song that claimed a good few minutes of screen time.

The percussive 'Crazy', which would remain otherwise unavailable, was memorable as much for the over-exuberant pogo dancing antics of Ian Hart's Liam (whom Marey had just ditched) as the performance itself. It did however give Clune the chance to spin his sticks and David the opportunity to wear an over the top gold shirt! 'Girl you really turn my head/I'm like a little kid jumping round my bed' are sample lyrics from this one, and when David was quizzed in a web conversation as to the song's availability he seemed not unhappy it wasn't easily obtainable.

Kathy Burke was called upon to sing her own version of 'Shine' over the closing credits of the film, and eventually did the job twice. Having insisted that she sings best when drunk, she recorded the song after a night on the town only to discover the next day that it sounded terrible! So she sang it sober in the end. David stood strumming alongside her, mouthing the words so intensely it was as if he was singing it himself. At the back of the deserted 'Three Fiddlers', the band's nose-ringed bass player looked on approvingly as he caught the singer's eye. It seemed he would be the next port of call on Marey's romantic merry-go-round. Although it had undoubtedly been a creative spur, *This Years Love* played no great role in gaining David Gray further recognition in his home country. "It's quite subtle, really," he'd reflect. "It's not like the film was about the music. It's brought me some attention and perhaps a little credibility but I don't think it moved any mountains."

When *Select* magazine accused him of acting, he responded in comically withering fashion. "You're actually flattering me there. I wish they'd given me a line, although I did have to do a meaningful look which I'm very proud of. I freeze frame it (on video) for everyone when they come round."

The new venture would be a departure from the past in every respect. With the exception of Clune, David had split with the musicians from the *Sell, Sell, Sell* era, meaning that Neil MacColl and long-time bassist/producer David Nolté were no longer on board. When asked what happened to Nolté, his response was a suitably inscrutable "much water flows under the bridge."

Nolté returned to the States and played bass with the Jigsaw Seen, as well as assisting brothers Joe and Mike whose latest version of The Last was recording for SST Records. He finally got a chance to indulge his anglophile roots when Kinks guitarist Dave Davies enrolled him in his Kink Kronikles band, supporting the main man on guitar and keyboards.

As well as involving just two musicians, the new venture would necessitate David Gray ditching – temporarily, at least – many of the songs he had débuted in the last few years. It seems that he wanted a cohesive collection, featuring a new vibe the existing songs did not have. It wasn't a question of grafting a new sound onto them, either: his new material was being created on instruments other than his standard acoustic guitar.

Such was the perceived break with what he had been doing for the past six years that Gray decided he would abandon working under his own name and call his partnership with Clune, the drummer, Silverado* – a group title that would not only recognise Clune's role as more than just a hired hand, but also break with his own unsuccessful solo past. In the event they decided against this, but used the receipts from two Irish tours – he was now able to sell out a 3,000-seat venue in Dublin and fill houses elsewhere – to buy new equipment. This included a drum machine, a sampler, a computer and a pair of effects units, all of which were installed at his home.

* The Lawrence Kasdan-directed western movie starring Kevin Kline and John Cleese.

Ironically, Gray's London gaff in Stoke Newington, N16 that now functioned as his recording studio was not that far from the house in nearby Haringey Travis had made their base in June 1996. Compared with those gung-ho Glaswegians whose street-gang mentality had kept them together in times of distress, Gray had ploughed a lone furrow: even Olivia had told him "you'll do well when you stop singing funny". Now, with Clune and a new sound, he may not have been Silverado but he was a band.

"It definitely was a collaborative thing. I involved Clune for a little while before the making of the record. We'd be grooving away somewhere in a rehearsal room, we'd tape it, develop the chords, and groove a bit more. We were just having fun, basically. We were starting songs from different things, from beats and bass-lines or from sounds I found on some of my synths. I'd find a weird sound and the song would grow out of that."

It's said that David Gray re-mortgaged his house to raise the money for recording equipment. "It was a bit grim, that's for sure," he admitted to MTV, "but what can you do? I wouldn't want to do it again, but you've just got to come through it. I sort of lost sight of why I was making music, as if it is something that's connected to the commercial world. But I thought, 'That's wrong; you just make music for music's sake.' When I got back on track with that, it all started going well."

Former producer Dave Anderson ran into him again at this point. "He was saying basically he was out of all his deals. He'd always been popular in Ireland fortunately which kept him going, and he decided to do this record completely by himself, buy some equipment. It was absolutely brilliant that he did it, confounded the music business by becoming a huge success without anyone A&Ring it at all."

But *White Ladder* wouldn't have happened in a regular studio/producer situation? "That's possibly true. Although obviously that came about because he was completely. . . he'd been dropped by everyone and that was his last throw of the dice. It's fantastic that he did it."

The lack of recording equipment – basically a computer and a couple of mics – would give the record its character. "You don't get any of that sort of really pristine £200,000 production," Gray admitted with a smile once it had all come right. And there was a huge change in his previously enclosed attitude towards the process of making music "It had become a little claustrophobic to sit there with a guitar with the weight of all my failings on me," he says. "I was sick of being the angsty singer-songwriter. I wanted to enjoy the music."

The opinions of his friends and family were canvassed on work in progress – so every time he and Clune came up with something, an impromptu *Juke Box Jury* would rate the results. "Clune would set up a groove, and I'd work on top of it," says Gray, "so I had a new way to write, which was really exciting. I'd play the embryonic ideas to my wife, my manager – basically I'd open myself up to criticism at a really early stage. You lose your insecurities and get stronger when other people are involved in the process."

There was also a definite absence of po-faced seriousness. "We did some things that I would have never had had the gall to do (before)," Gray recalled. "We were going, 'Hey, how about a really cheesy house bass line?' and then going for it, involving sound in a much more interesting way and not just sounding like a derivative of a Bob Dylan band."

Unforeseen problems with home recording included a rogue cat, which Gray claims was directly responsible for breaking two different pieces of equipment by climbing onto a keyboard balanced on top of another keyboard and bringing both down. The neighbours, too, were understandably unhappy if recording went on beyond a certain time, even if their vacuum cleaner had been an occasional unwelcome intruder on sessions.

Drums and percussion in particular were guaranteed to bring extra sound effects like banging on the wall, so with typical resourcefulness David and Clune borrowed an acquaintance's photographic studio to record the drums for the whole album – in one go! There was only one fly in the ointment. The photographer who'd said they could use it had neglected to tell his assistant. Gray: "We were trying to record drums and he was trying to do a shoot. We got so sick of waiting for them that we just did the take anyway. So we were recording drums and you can hear the photographer clicking away on the other side. We had to snip out bits where the phone would ring."

The drums were set up on one side of the room, and the photographer's assistant had his models in the other – there was also a film being filmed on the floor above. "So we were doing these stupid, stupid takes, like, 'He's having a cup of tea right now, come on, play the music, fucking tape it!' It was mad, but it also hung together, it seemed to make sense. We managed to hang on to what we were doing the whole time."

Engineer Iestyn Polson would later reveal to studio magazine *Sound On Sound* that the drum parts Clune performed in this unsympathetic environment were captured on just two microphones – one recording the sound of the room, the other pointing directly at the bass drum. "The whole drum track on the album was recorded like that, in mono. You could put up the fader (on the mixing desk) and that was the drum sound."

The home recording sessions worked in a pattern. Clune would start by setting up a groove, programming a beat into the drum machine, and David would come up with ideas over the top of it. The multi-talented percussionist would then devise a bass line before the sampler became involved – all of this alchemy being captured by Polson. "It's something we'd been moving towards slowly since before *Sell, Sell, Sell*," Gray would explain. "We'd been experimenting with things and it just gelled by *White Ladder*. We didn't try to take old songs and clamp the technology onto them, we came up with a load of new stuff which was born at the same time as the beat or the sample or whatever. It was an organic process."

The big advantage was not that this didn't sound like anything David Gray had done before – it didn't really sound like anything any of his heroes had done, either. "It's very difficult to get away from a Bob Dylan and a Van Morrison sound when you've got an acoustic guitar and a piano and a drum kit. They've done so much with that. But this was a funny noise or an odd beat or whatever – it just sounded like us." The occasional bit of traffic noise through the open windows of his living room just added to the charm.

The album's sound was distinctly low-fi for much of the time. "Working at home in that way is a much more relaxed environment; you're not watching the clock tick down at a thousand pounds a day. You're just sitting there doing the vocal on a chair and the cat's sitting next to you and the window's open and the telly's on in the next room. There's a completely different vibe and I think that's good."

The duo were creating right onto recording tape (or, more accurately if less romantically, hard disc), a freshness reflected in tracks like 'We're Not Right' and 'Babylon' which had literally never been performed in that way before. It was a total contrast to the usual 'take 28' mentality of most acts whose creativity fails to flow in state-of-the-art recording studios.

They would carry on recording even when people came round; Gray claims the evidence is there to be picked up by sharp-eared listeners. "With 'Babylon', there's loads of people there coughing away and farting or whatever. It was chaos," he admitted, "but that felt more interesting, richer, than the classic 'alone on the studio with headphones on' vibe. It was a ridiculously haphazard recording process, fraught with technical problems, but it was quite nice to be making a record in that anarchic way."

"When you go into big studios," he told VH1, "what you actually get is posh productions and that makes every record sound similar, unless you're an absolute genius about how to use the desk. We didn't feel comfortable with 2,000 knobs and 400 pieces of outboard gear. So we didn't have anything really to play with, all we had was the sound we made and a few limited textures. That was enough. There's a spirit and softness to the record; it's really mellow. It was a very understated dynamic. We couldn't strive for a big sound. And that can be surprisingly powerful."

Gray's fans may not have been great in number at this point, but the advent of the Internet gave them the means to share their mania. The virtual rumour mill had resounded with suggestions about the eventual name of the record. Everyone was agreed on the first word of the title, but suggestions had included *White Letters*, *White Landing* and even *White Elephant*. Anyone looking backwards would have found a giant clue in the lyrics to 'Everytime' from *Sell, Sell, Sell*, which included the line 'Your spine a white ladder'.

The album was considerably less guitar-driven than its predecessor, however, with drum-machines and samples evident throughout giving it almost a dance feel. That said, David's traditional strengths of thought-provoking lyrics and memorable melodies still shone through.

The transformation was likened by some to that enjoyed by Everything But The Girl, the duo of Tracy Thorn and Ben Watt, who'd hit on a successful formula almost by accident when their 'Missing' was turned from contemporary folk-song to dance anthem (and a transatlantic Top Three single, to boot) by a handy Todd Terry remix. Others cite the Beastie Boys' 'Paul's Boutique', one of the definitive hip hop albums of its time that was light-years away from its predecessor and recorded for 1989 release under their own auspices between spells at Def Jam and Capitol.

David himself cited Beth Orton and Beck as artists he admired for bringing technology and songwriting together. He certainly approved of the effect this new approach was having on his music, even though he'd never seen his material as a soundtrack to buy jeans by. "You could imagine it in clothes shops as you're picking out your new garment! In a way, it's more contemporary," he concluded. "I think it's lighter, more palatable. It's quite an intimate thing but the lightness shouldn't fool anyone into thinking that there's not as much nourishment in it. It's been framed differently so it's more accessible, not so intense. You need new stuff to come into your musical cocktail every now and again. I was just looking for some way to make it more interesting for me.

"With Clune experimenting, over quite a long period of time, with a new sort of sound, and working at home with Clune in a different way, and suddenly realising that it was working. I was using Clune to collaborate with, so things had a different feel. I wasn't sitting alone in a dark room with my guitar, weaving tales of misery. I was having a bit of a laugh, really – heaven forbid – with Clune, and we were using samples and drum machines and it was really exciting, yet it was working."

It was clear from the percussive nature of the new music that Clune was the fulcrum around which everything turned: in live performance, his kit would be set up at right angles to the front-line musicians rather than at the back, allowing the crucial interplay between himself and Gray full rein. Yet despite his flamboyant manner, he seemed to shun publicity. "He is Clune and Clune only," Gray says. "Like Cher or Madonna. He has a very similar temperament, actually, but I think he has worse body odour than they do."

David Gray's move to found his own label to release the new album was a reflection of his feelings after previous record deals had gone awry. But it was a calculated risk. Electro-pop pioneer Gary Numan had taken the same step in 1984, forming Numa Records with his father's help and assistance – yet the whole thing had proved both expensive and time consuming. Not only had the expenditure of time diverted Gary's attention from the music, with self-confessed damaging results, but he was still feeling the financial wounds years after he'd cut his losses and signed to another label. Fortunately that would not be the case with David Gray. He had the advantage of an increasing commercial momentum, whereas Numan's was declining from an early-Eighties peak.

White Ladder, then, was an album that "owes as much to the sampler as the acoustic guitar, more to the computer than the tape machine." All the old rules about what a folk-based singer/songwriter should be doing were obliterated, and with them David Gray's past, inauspicious, three-album career. And the change was more than obvious the moment the opening piano chords, synth washes and drum beats of 'Please Forgive Me' burst forth.

This was a song that had "just sort of tumbled down in half an hour" after Gray wrote the first line. "I do love it when that happens; it doesn't happen very often." He had come up with the chords while messing around on his keyboard and thought, "Oh, I got something here. . . It seems like a very simple song – not so much about falling in love for the first time, but re-falling in love. It's a love song tempered by experience, but almost more passionate for the rediscovery."

Gray attributes the passion of his vocal to the fact that this was one of the first times he'd sung the song properly. "You get into a moment with live music and that's how it should be in the studio. I think 'Please Forgive Me' has exactly that." It wasn't simply a great dance track, though. According to Gray, "People use the song to get over their break-ups: it's a reliable piece of emotion that you can touch base with. There's melancholy there but it's a comforting thing to have around, like talking to a friend. We've all been through stuff that's gone wrong."

The 'lightning running through veins' metaphor has become a much-cherished one by Gray fans trying to explain the attraction of his music. The introduction of the acoustic guitar hook and the falling away of the musical backdrop leaving piano and voice before a dance-orientated coda brought the guitar back was very much a dance number's formula.

'Please Forgive Me' was "already quite a dancy track" according to its writer, but would be made "much more dancy" by Paul Hartnoll of Orbital. While admitting to being "fascinated by what people will do in a re-mix", the writer had no qualms about his music being tampered with. "It's become an expected part of music culture at the moment," he shrugged

Next came 'Babylon', the track that would come to represent David Gray to many people and certainly introduce him to the majority of his current fan base. But when you refer to 'Babylon', you open a Pandora's box of possibilities. For as well as the original version on the original album release, 'Babylon' would appear twice as a UK single, each time having large sections re-recorded and remixed.

Though the piano played an important part in the appeal of the song, careful attention to the album and single versions of 'Babylon' will reveal crucial differences. The album version has much more piano from the start and echo piano with a left/right delay on the verses, as well as a vocoder-effect piano which the trio of Gray, Clune and Polson got bored with and decided to remove for the single. "Every time we put up the fader the first thing you'd hear would be 'dang, dang dang a-dang'," said the engineer, "and we wanted to hear something different." The Roland piano used on the album was replaced by a "much more pleasant-sounding" Kawai instrument.

The piano was now exclusively used on the choruses of the single version, while an extra guitar part that comes in at the start of the second verse "to lift the song". It's possible to hear traffic rumble on that sample, but fortunately the engineer likes noise – "it adds character."

"My favourite bit," he continued, "is the wacky guitar thing that comes in right at the end of the song. That's an acoustic guitar loop, edited, then put through a North Pole plug-in resonant filter. It's a tiny bit of that first guitar motif from the beginning of the song, bounced out through the digital bounce page."

Unusually, the double-tracked vocal harmony that follows David's lead part in the chorus sections is not the lead singer double-tracked but Clune. The singing drummer recorded his part in same photographic studio as he did the drums, "but that time," Polson revealed, "we used the darkroom bit, which was better acoustically for vocals than the big, echoey concrete room."

To Gray, 'Babylon' was and is "just a simple, little pop song," but when questioned further he'll admit it contained "a lot of feeling from a period when things hadn't been going so well for me. I was questioning my relationship (and) just about everything else as well. So I think there's a lot of emotion from my period of doubt that are kind of in the song."

That said, the music came first, as with all the *White Ladder* selections. "If I come up with something, I might start singing something along with it, and then I'll do the lyrics later," he says. "I'll try to keep as much of what I was singing originally as I can, because I prefer the instinctive feel of things, even if it doesn't make complete sense."

Turning 'Babylon' into a single would take three weeks, during which the strings were re-recorded, the song was edited down and the drums re-done. The guitar hook which is reminiscent of the chorus was moved forward to make more of a starting point, but the major problem was the tuning on the track. Apparently, the guitar Gray was using was not perfectly in tune with itself, requiring much dextrous use of studio technology to make the re-recorded strings sound right with it.

He'd forsaken his usual Martin instrument for an Irish guitar, a Lowden, he'd bought round about the time he'd started making repeated trips to that country. "Though it's battered and bruised by my brutal treatment it's got a really sweet sound," he told *Guitar World Acoustic* magazine in 2001. Yet in other interviews David had claimed to regard it as a mere tool of the trade. "I've got a few guitars, I don't have any names for them. I like the ones that are old and battered and they sound good. I think when guitars are worn in and beaten up they have a more interesting character and sound to them.

"I don't like people who fuss over their instruments," he continued, warming to his theme. "Mine gets all dented and broken. I feel like it's more of a friend when it's had a few knocks. The thing is, when you get successful, you suddenly get all these new instruments. They time it so that the moment you can afford to buy the stuff you've always wanted, that's when they give it to you for nothing. So they're going to have to impress me with their individual characters."

The Lowden had not found favour when he first bought it, and had remained in its case until another instrument broke on a tour. "I had to start using the Lowden as a main guitar and it's been very, very good. It's very boomy, with a massive body on it."

'Babylon's bass line, taken off a Roland MC303 groovebox, was also simplified in the verse, allowing a shift from rhythm to melody. "It becomes more light-hearted," explained engineer Polson, adding "It's nice to have some musical relief after the chorus has been banging away."

If old-time David Gray fans were looking for a reference point, a song that might have come from one of the earlier albums, then track three, 'My Oh My', was probably the nearest thing. Surprisingly, perhaps, this would be the first of three songs on the album to credit Clune as co-writer. The synthesised strings were in the background as the vocal was very much the focus. Gray's diction was now much improved from the early days, when a lyric sheet for reference was almost obligatory. Spitting out words like 'de-fi-nite', his delivery was now definitive.

Though its writer admits is was "inspired by drunken excess", 'We're Not Right' was one of the album's quieter moments. "We worked out a bit of theory, we decided the rock thing was not happening. The Americans liked it, but I said it sounded shit. We should abandon all attempts at rocking. The intimate songs are the moments in the gig when we've really got people." The combination of low, farting bass line, slap percussion and thin synthesiser solo was a unique one

The stark, solo-intro'd 'Nightblindness' was added to the album in its re-issued form, having found popularity both as a B-side and a live number. It contained an obligatory clock/time reference, in this case 'twenty five past eternity', while posing the question so many couples ask at the beginning of another cash-strapped month: 'what we gonna do when the money runs out?'

The easy delivery was deliberate. "Rock was out, as far as we were concerned. We weren't going to kerrang anymore or overstate anything. We were going to find other ways around the music. The

groove seemed to work much better than an electric guitar or a heavily hit drum as far as getting a point across. It allowed a lot of space
for the words and the chords. It never interfered."

The attitude carried over to 'Silver Lining', at six minutes one of
the longer selections. Its economical use of words seemed to suggest
he'd finally mastered something he'd suggested back in 1994 when he
told journalist Colin Harper that "words is what I'm into, but to get
further into words doesn't necessarily mean using more of them. I see
that economy is all. You can say a lot with a few sentences. A bluesman can put a lot of suffering into a few clichés, but if he sings them
right and maybe just tweaks the odd word in here or there – a weird
word that you wouldn't expect – suddenly you've got this kind of
classic, you know what I mean? They're an interesting case in point,
because they know what they're trying to get into their song, but
they don't extend their word play very far." The phrase 'Scatter it like
diamonds all across these lands' could well be a reflection of that
unusual inspiration.

'White Ladder', the album's uptempo title track, was one of the
quickest to come together, the vocals being committed to tape the
morning after the backing track had been completed. Gray had used
dummy words for the run-through and admits the singing, including
the nearest to a falsetto he would attempt, "was done not knowing
what I was doing: this is important. I was feeling for it reaching for it
and that's what you get at a good gig. You can't go back and do it
again, you're forcing, you're always going forward." The sounds, he
concluded, "had been knocking on my ears for so long but I realised
the songs had to grow out of the samples."

Having sworn off the "two electric guitars, thrashing away," David
had returned to the keyboard for inspiration, and there were a number of songs that clearly benefited from that. "When I write on the
keyboard I'm open to so much more melody," he'd said. There's more
space to chords, and that leaves more room for the drums, bass or
whatever. So a groovier kind of beat is more applicable."

'This Year's Love' was one of those songs. Clearly inspired by the
film of the same name, it stood up quite satisfactorily on its own. The
lyrics, complete with clichés like 'cuts like a knife' and 'sweep me off
my feet', may not have stood close inspection, but the musical flow

took the listener along with it. This, like Van Morrison's *Astral Weeks*, was an album to submerge yourself in, an album where the whole was greater than the sum of the parts just as the songs were more than the sum of lyrics and music.

'Sail Away' was *Mojo* magazine's choice of outstanding song – "a lush ballad wherein some deep, rumbling percussion and a soaring chord progression really do evoke images of boats sailing off into the wild blue yonder." Starting simply with guitar, voice and rhythm, it builds imperceptibly to include keyboard and strings. But even then there was none of the over-elaboration of an Elton John or Moody Blues, either of whom could quite conceivably have performed the song. To take things further, the whistling that concluded the track could as easily have been bearded middle of the road croonster Roger Whittaker of 'Durham Town' fame or Bryan Ferry in 'Jealous Guy' mode, but the undercurrent of the 'funky drummer' beat beloved of the likes of George Michael kept the track determinedly contemporary. Incidentally, a phrase from this song's lyric, "I've been talking drunken gibberish", became the name of one of Gray's fan websites.

The choice of Soft Cell's 'Say Hello Wave Goodbye' was one many remarked on. It was also surprising that it should have made the transformation from stage favourite to album track. "There's something dreadfully dull about doing a Bob Dylan cover, for example," he explained to VH1. "Why should I do that? It's already obvious that I loved him. . . it's far nicer to turn something on its head. I'm always on the lookout for something ridiculous that no one would dream of covering, like 'Careless Whisper' by George Michael. But I'm rather drawn to these Eighties ballads. I'm betraying my teenage nostalgia.

"Anyway, I was stuck for a cover one night, doing some kind of charity gig or something. And from the moment I first played it, everyone started singing along, because no one had heard it for so long, and it was such a different way of doing it as well. It just took on a life of its own."

'Say Hello, Wave Goodbye' saw him drop phrases of two classic Van Morrison songs, 'Into the Mystic' and 'Madam George' into the lyrics. He must have passed the notoriously hard to please Irishman's test because the credits reveal that this was done with permission.

Gray was more than pleased with the results of his one and only recorded cover version. "Sometimes you sing a song and nothing really happens, but other times you get right into it. It's as if that one was written for me. It seemed to take on a life of its own. And it seemed fitting with the whole mood of the record. It's a goodbye to that style of things 'cos that track's more like what I've been doing for the past five years."

White Ladder had begun with a surprise hidden track, presumably titled 'Can't Get Through To Myself'. This required track one to be selected before rewinding a minute or so. Its Dylanesque free association 'New leather jacket and a helium voice/my head is reeling through too much choice' made it sound like a *Flesh/Sell, Sell, Sell* out-take and certainly not a *White Ladder* candidate.

Perhaps the most curious rumour about *White Ladder* to sweep the internet was that every track on the album concerned heroin. Condemning the notion as "ludicrous", Gray did admit to *Select* that he had indulged in ecstasy "when I used to go to Orbital gigs... it was part of the package. I tried it again recently (mid-2000) but it wasn't really me. My head moves way too fast without any fucking E."

The whole procedure had given David Gray the direct involvement in and control over the recording process he'd always yearned for. Suddenly the frustrations of creating his earlier albums and working with outside producers were in the past. "I've always been a ridiculously stubborn person, I wouldn't accept any wanky producer bollocks. It's like someone trying to dress you. It's like 'go away, I know I'll find the trousers somewhere that I'm after!' And eventually I did. It just took a long time.

"I'd always tried to do everything live, but this was even better because we had a backing track that was completely synched up and you could change it afterwards. You had what you needed and could tamper subtly with what was going on in the background at your leisure - which is perfect, because it's capturing that performance moment that is the most difficult thing. It allowed me to be as raw and spontaneous as I wanted to be on top, I'd perform songs live which is what the ear is drawn to first, and then all the stuff behind it can be produced after the event."

And production of the raw material would take some while, battling against the limited technology they enjoyed. A Soundcraft

6000 mixing desk was borrowed "from a mate" to mix the album, but the power supply on the computer was buzzing all the time. Gray, Polson and Clune were working with the maximum number of audio tracks possible with the computer drive, so it was a toss–up whether the computer would overload before the mixing of the song had been finished.

To make matters worse, workmen had been digging up the road outside the house while they were trying to do the vocals. "It was a nightmare," Polson sighed. "The album was cobbled together, believe me!" Little did they realise at the time, but this cobbled–together album was about to take the world by storm. . .

CHAPTER 6

Selling *White Ladder*

The new album finished, taking the music to the people was the next step. And as he awaited the release of what would become his breakthrough album, the summer of 1998 was to see David Gray reborn on the open-air stages of Britain and Ireland. Wherever there was a festival you could almost guarantee he'd be there.

The Fleadh '98 in London's Finsbury Park in June was typical. Once a celebration of music from the Emerald Isle, the open-air festival had broadened its musical policy considerably (and would continue to do so: 2001 would find the definitely non-Celtic Neil Young headlining). But it was certain David Gray's Irish connections hadn't proved any hindrance to obtaining an invite.

As a lesser-known artist, David was not considered worthy to grace the main stage but was cloistered away in the *Time Out* tent. Yet from the moment he hit the stage with just the inevitable Clune in tow, the omens were good – even if they'd had to set up their own gear unassisted! The marquee crowd had been warmed up by folkies Equation and then Ghostland, Sinead O'Connor's backing band, who performed a set of their own before returning to end the evening's entertainment (on that particular stage, at least) with their patron. Both early acts won enthusiastic applause, but Gray and Clune's impact with just a single acoustic guitar and drum kit would prove every bit as popular.

That said, they were entertaining an audience necessarily unfamiliar with their work. You'd have had to have been a convert from earliest days to recognise the opening 'Living Room' from *A Century Ends*, but its uptempo nature and copious references to "heads full of beer" made it a more than appropriate choice for the Guinness-sponsored (and fuelled) festival. Gray both saluted and took the mickey out of the occasion, climbing on to the drum riser to perform a mock 'stadium rock band' ending.

This well received opener was followed by 'The Light', stand-out track from *Flesh*, which enabled long-time fans in the by now sizeable audience to identify themselves by singing lustily along. A new, mid-paced song, 'Nightblindness' – a B-side that would find a place on the re-vamped *White Ladder* – faded out in stately fashion rather than stopping abruptly, leaving the as-yet unfamiliar audience uncertain exactly when to applaud ("that was definitely a *moment*," he quipped, clearly enjoying himself).

The odd audience requests for early material (like *Flesh*'s 'New Horizons') were brushed off in favour of another newie, 'Sail Away', from *White Ladder*.* But time on this particular day was necessarily short, a *Time Out* tent slot being limited to not much more than half an hour. Accordingly, 'Say Hello, Wave Goodbye' was chosen to close the truncated set – and won Gray and Clune an unpredicted standing ovation, the like of which neither of the preceding acts had managed to inspire.

After this small victory and with *White Ladder*'s imminent release in mind, it was back to the familiarity of Ireland where, as a headlining act, David had more time and thus more scope to entertain. He had now been able to re-employ the services of ex-The Fat Lady Sings man Tim Bradshaw who, since their earlier touring together, had played with the likes of Tom Robinson, Tanita Tikaram, Nan Vernon and Fatima Mansions. As well as guitar, his accomplishments included

---

* Staggering to relate, this would be released as a 'new single' exactly three years later!

keyboards, drums and backing vocals, making him an ideal foil for a front man flitting between guitar and piano.

Galway's Black Box Theatre played host to Gray as July closed and, while he now had assistance on keyboards/guitar as well as Clune in the engine room, it was certain Gray would have had theatregoers eating out of the palm of his hand had he been up there with no more than his battered acoustic guitar for company.

The crowd were on their feet straight way as *A Century Ends*'s 'Living Room' was this time followed by *Flesh*'s 'Falling Free' – both songs everyone in the house knew and loved by now. It was then deemed time to introduce the as-yet unheard 'Sail Away', which received a positive reception. Interestingly, he was unwilling to over-whelm the crowd with too many songs they'd yet to encounter.

As it transpired, though, these few months would see the final per-formances of some old favourites. The set continued with 'New Horizons' and 'Debauchery' before the pace slowed with the first album's reflective 'Gathering Dust'. That having been well received, David judged it time to unveil two more new compositions 'Heartland Of Mystery' and 'So Far Away'. Surprisingly, neither of these were to appear on the album his listeners had yet to experience. . . but on the night that didn't diminish his audience's appreciation.

Time for the snarling 'What Are You', always a crowd-pleaser since it kicked off *Flesh*, 'Smile' (surprisingly the first sell *Sell, Sell, Sell* selec-tion of the evening), and two more new ones, 'Silver Lining' and 'Babylon'. The audience became slightly subdued as 'Lead Me Upstairs' was followed by two more new songs, 'I Can't Make It On My Own' (still currently unreleased) and 'As I'm Leaving' (which made it onto 'Lost Songs' two years on).

In the words of reviewer Colman Duffy, "We were watching a man explore his personal life on a very public stage. The experi-ence was awesome. It seemed to become a communal exploration as the audience became totally concentrated on the music and the singer."

'Late Night Radio' from his third album had become something of a staple on Irish radio, and the house erupted when he turned up the volume on his acoustic guitar to lead the band into a storming ver-sion. The main set having ended with 'It's All Over', the trio left the stage to a rolling wave of applause. 'The Light' and 'Say Hello, Wave Goodbye' ended proceedings as encores.

When it was finally time to let *White Ladder* out into the world. David would reward his hard-core Irish fans by letting them be first to sample its delights. His fourth, but first self-financed effort was released on 13 November 1998 on his own label, IHT Records ("It's HIT messed up," he explains), distributed by the Irish label Grapevine. An initial 4,000 copies of the album were pressed, funded in part with £9,000 Gray had accidentally been overpaid by his new song publisher, Chrysalis Music. "There was a real thrill," says Gray of the moment the discs were shipped off to Ireland. "You could just sense something good started to happen." The albums sold out, and they pressed 5,000 more.

Soon Irish radio, which had been leaked a few advance tracks in the weeks leading up to the launch, caught on to 'Babylon', and manager Holden's later revelation that they'd "felt incredibly reckless putting out 4,000 copies" of the album began to seem on the timid side. As support came from both national and local stations, Gray and his band gigged their way from city to city in an effort to enlarge his small but dedicated fanbase. Word of mouth was crucial, and even if they could have afforded a saturation advertising campaign it's doubtful Gray and company would have used the tactic.

"Everyone who was working the record, everyone involved, was really enjoying it and that's infectious," he explained. "They all felt a part of something that's going on. People are used to being served things through the media and devouring them. This was something they felt maybe they'd discovered. They'd felt a part of it."

If anyone was expecting a backlash such as Bob Dylan had faced when he controversially 'went electric;' at 1965's Newport Folk Festival, then it was Gray himself. "There was a bit of that, but we were expecting much more, to be honest. It was a radical departure for me. It's not a radical record by anybody's standards, but (it is) compared to what I've done before. There's beats, there's drum machines all the way through, really. That was brilliant, because the way we were working, you couldn't drum and we couldn't do all those things. We had to find other ways and means of doing it, so we started out with just a beatbox, and then we did a bit of drumming in some

89

way and sampled it. It sounded great. There was a bit of a backlash, but Christ, we thought there was going to be hundreds of people: "This is terrible. What have we done?" You know, especially 'cause the first track on the album, 'Please Forgive Me', is particularly. . . it's got a slight cheesy kind of pop element to it. But no one seemed to really give a shit."

Though no longer in the picture, former sideman David Nolté could see the progression – and was not only delighted with the results but keen to ensure the credit was shared between the singer and his longest-serving collaborator. "The biggest difference between *White Ladder* and the three previous records is Clune's influence. The beats you hear are 100 per cent Clune. He was always playing that way when we'd rehearse and we would mess around with it a little, but then go right back to our 'straight and normal' way of playing. When Dave made *White Ladder*, he had no one telling him how he should sound, he had nothing to lose by experimenting with what had become a formula and, by collaborating with Clune, he finally found the right backdrop for his songs."

In Ireland, particularly, David Gray had been portrayed as the outsider whose talent had triumphed over the machinations of the music business. Now here he was being pushed as a new 'priority act' by East West. As it would transpire, however, any die-hards the record would lose Gray were more than outnumbered by new converts. "The people who have bought the record are people who haven't participated in a long time," Gray says, explaining the appeal of *White Ladder*. "It's got melody and a strong spirit. I'm quite the opposite of cynical – the music is real, the emotion is real and the sentiments are heartfelt. When people come to see us they seem to bring a positive energy with them. Perhaps there aren't many other outlets for that right now."

Due to its début in Ireland fully 18 months before it hit the UK on a major label, *White Ladder* would have the chance to infiltrate the consciousness of Gray's home nation by stealth. It had some influential fans on its side from the off: Radio 1's Mark Radcliffe and new music guru Jo Whiley had already voiced their approval. But when he returned to the capital, his current home city, in September '98 to play for the first time since the Finsbury Park Fleadh, it wasn't the

David, photographed backstage at Glastonbury, in 2000. *(LFI)*

Without whom… David's main influences are Sixties era Bob Dylan (top left), *Astral Weeks* era Van Morrison (top right), The Waterboys' Mike Scott (bottom left) and Smiths era Morrissey (bottom right).
(LFI; Peter Anderson/SIN)

David on stage at the 2000 Glastonbury Festival. *(LFI)*

David Gray with David Nolté, who produced *Sell, Sell, Sell,* and has played guitar and bass with Gray on several tours. *(Courtesy David Nolté)*

Dave Anderson, who guided David Gray through his first single and studio album *A Century Ends*. *(Courtesy of Steven Budd Management)*

The Bible in 1988, featuring guitarist Neill MacColl (extreme left) who played guitar on David's first two albums.

David on stage at Shepherds Bush Empire, August 2000. *(All Action)*

Dave Matthews, the South African born musician transplanted to the US who gave David his US record deal and generally encouraged his career. *(LFI)*

David Gray at the *Q* magazine awards in London, 2001. *(All Action)*

David on piano at the Party In The Park, in London's Hyde Park, 2001. *(Rex)*

David on stage at the V2001 Festival. *(Rex)*

"Most of my songs are lit by the wonder of being alive. Even if that means feeling blue. Ultimately you do, as a singer, want to transport people, make that connection." *(Redferns)*

Hammersmith Apollo or Shepherds Bush Empire David Gray would find himself gracing but Dingwalls at Camden Lock – the same venue he'd opened for Joan Baez five years earlier and just a step up the road from the *This Year's Love* neighbourhood. Maybe, instead of reflecting how far he hadn't progressed, he was aware he could still have been backing Kathy Burke in the pub!

Taking the mickey from the off with his own self-introduction – "Ladies and Gentleman, live on stage. . . David Gray," he was surprised to find more than a few fans in the audience. They'd have noticed the addition of keyboards to the act, and would have found the likes of 'Babylon' and 'Sail Away' fairly new to them. Not so, of course, 'Debauchery', which was introduced by Gray thus: "For those of you who know who the hell I am, this is from my first record. . ."

Unusually he'd opened with 'Its All Over', though the other perennial set-closer 'Say Hello, Wave Goodbye' (introduced, in the spirit of the evening, as "one Marc Almond wrote for me") went down predictably well. Though he didn't play it that night, Gray had recently introduced another cover into his set. 'Pale Blue Eyes' was an old Lou Reed/Velvet Underground song, too old and/or obscure to be recognised by most of his fans.

As the world prepared to ease itself into 1999, *White Ladder* steadfastly refused to leave the Irish charts. 'This Year's Love' and Babylon' had already been released as singles, boosting the album's profile still further, and more roadwork was followed by a sold out 4,500-capacity headline gig at the Big Beat Festival in Galway in July. This only served to emphasise David's meteoric rise and brought the album into the Irish Top Five – a full eleven months after release.

At Glastonbury he'd occupy a well-received early afternoon spot in the New Bands tent. He'd witnessed his all-time favourite concert in the shadow of the Tor nearly a decade and a half earlier when The Cure were caught in a lightning storm. "Ever since I first went to Glastonbury, I think in 1985, and I saw the bands playing on the main stage, I've thought 'I've got to do this'. It's the best place ever to do a gig."

There'd be a few competitors for gig of the summer. August brought a performance at Slane Castle which found David down the bill to Stereophonics and bill-topper Robbie Williams. The former Bad Boy of Take That was broadcast as it happened on pay per view television, attracting much controversy for his four-letter outbursts and buttock-baring, and though the bottom line was that the ebullient and predominantly adolescent 80,000 crowd had come to see Robbie, David's performance (which sadly did not receive as much exposure as Robbie's rear) was warmly received. Also, David's Slane warm-up gig at Dublin's HQ venue had sold out in 48 hours, leading to a second date – a morale-boosting exercise in its own right.

Everything was set up, then, for a full Irish tour in December 1999, culminating in that astonishing gig at the Point Depot on 22 December. The Millennium celebrations then intervened, but many a new fan must have braved their hangover, dashed out and spent their record tokens on *White Ladder* as, by mid January 2000, it had begun a five-week stint at Number One and would maintain a position in the Top 10 throughout the forthcoming year. But that was the future.

And that was Ireland. In Britain, he was still playing stand-up venues to a few hundred people, like the Wedgewood Rooms in Portsmouth in November '99. Though *Hants Chronicle* reviewer Oliver Gray had bought *White Ladder* in its original version and was aware of the forthcoming Point Depot show, he was still a lone voice in the wilderness. "It was one of those gigs where you only realised how much you enjoyed it after the event was over, perhaps due to the difficulty of generating an atmosphere in a half-empty hall." It could have been worse: Oliver Gray had seen his namesake playing a year earlier as a guitar and vocal solo act at Southampton's Joiner's Arms, to an even smaller audience, and hence had not bothered reviewing him.

His review continued: "An unlikely-looking pop star (he looks a lot like the comedian Graham Norton), Gray's strengths are the power of his songs and his voice, plus a willingness to throw out a no-holds-barred performance. Marketed as a male version of Beth Orton (ie folkie goes electronic), he really is at his best when abandoning his acoustic guitar and really going for radio-friendliness, as in the superb single 'Please Forgive Me'." The review's closing sentence would prove prescient. "If David Gray pursues this direction, tickets will be harder to find next time around."

While he continued playing to a relatively apathetic home audience, Gray had a double confidence booster. As *White Ladder* passed the triple platinum mark in Ireland, he received the coveted *Hot Press* 'Guest of the Nation' award, beating off the likes of fellow 'foreigners' Robbie Williams (revenge was sweet) and R.E.M. Keeping his trousers firmly buckled, "It's been an amazing year," he admitted, "beyond any of our expectations. Having had no proven track record of commercial success, I would hardly have been expecting to get a triple platinum (album)."

But the intimacy of old would henceforth become a memory as he moved on to bigger things. "Things have got to change for us and the fans," he conceded. "The situation has changed. It's moved on a few paces, so we're just trying to keep things interesting. You can't please all the people all the time. We wanted to have a big party (at the Point) and get the most amount of people as we could at it. If the gig in Galway hadn't gone so well this summer I don't think we would have contemplated it. That gig had four and a half thousand people and that was just a riot so we thought what the hell – why not play the Point?"

As for creativity, he'd hardly written a song all year because he'd been too busy. When the year ends which I'm really looking forward to, I'm planning to chill out, take a bit of time out and let the whole writing process start. I think I've had all of 1999 I can take for now."

He'd finished off the year with a 'new' single, 'Please Forgive Me', the video for which was A-listed on MTV UK and Ireland. The opening track of the album was now to receive the remix treatment from Paul Hartnoll, the Orbital connection enabling it to bag the coveted Record of the Week slot on Radio 1's *Essential Selection* show hosted by influential DJ Pete Tong – which in turn ensured it massive exposure in Ibiza and on London's club scene.

The music business is well known for its revolving door policy that sees people playing musical chairs and flitting from company to company. It was this kind of internal politics that had dogged Gray's career up until now, and he was probably glad to be out of it. After all *White Ladder*, on its initial UK 'indie' release, would clock up a respectable 20,000 sales. Yet no matter how creditable that was, it was clear that without more muscle *White Ladder* would remain short of fulfilling its potential. It was significant, then, when Christian Tattersfield, who shared an Orbital connection with Rob Holden, took charge of EastWest, a subsidiary of US giant Warner Brothers. As an interested observer of the story so far, Tattersfield was convinced that, if his new label applied its muscle, *White Ladder* could replicate its Irish success in Britain.

Tattersfield's background was in dance music, having been the A&R man for the Systematic label. One of his signings, Anglo-Italian duo Alex Party, had risen as high as Number Two. Next stop had been Decca/London's ffrr imprint, an altogether bigger proposition, where Orbital had been one of his charges. Whether he was attracted by the 'house bass-lines' and dance trappings of *White Ladder* is uncertain, but he undoubtedly saw potential.

Having achieved Irish success on his own terms and his own label, Gray was, for the first time in his performing and recording life, able to call the shots. He was ready to deal with the major-label record business again and licensed *White Ladder* to EastWest Records in the UK when they promised "to do for you in Britain what you've done for yourself in Ireland."

The promise was one Tattersfield would be given the chance to fulfil. "It's the perfect deal for me because it still gives me creative control over everything," said David, "Running my own label was denying me time to concentrate on my songwriting and this allows me to get back to doing what I really want to do."

But he wouldn't have given up an ounce of his hard-won freedom for just anybody. "If it hadn't been for Christian," Gray continued, "I would never have even entertained the idea of signing. But he persuaded me with his brutal logic and his enormous budget! He wants to sell a million records, he wants me to win the Brit Awards, he has incredible objectives. But he also didn't waffle on with the psychological 'I love you' stuff. He just talked the hard facts: 'This is going to work. What else is there out there?'"

The deal went through on 12 April 2000, the label wasting no time in re-releasing *White Ladder* on the first of the following month. A major marketing push was set to coincide, with tour dates planned through until October. EastWest duly took full-page ads for the album in several leading music and style magazines. Soon, publications which had ignored the album on its initial release were giving it house room – and rave reviews. (*The Daily Telegraph's* Neil McCormick, an Irishman, pronounced, "this could be my album of the year".)

With Gray's rapidly rising profile came increased airplay – and sales. By early June, *White Ladder* was hovering around the mid-teens on the UK album chart, the video for 'Babylon' was popping up regularly on MTV and requests for TV and live appearances were coming in thick and fast. An album its maker had derided as being "something for nothing and next to nothing (done) by the book" had come up trumps. And the key to it all would be 'Babylon'.

When it had been selected for release as a single first time round, the clearest weak point in the production of the song was the drum sound. Hence Clune had re-recorded his parts during a half-day session at Mylow Studios. This was just the start of a Frankenstein's monster-style reconstruction that would take the song and its performance a long way from its humble bedsitter beginnings. The vocal had also been changed while editing the song down for the first time. The dynamics of the choruses didn't work, according to engineer Iestyn Polson, "so we redid some vocals just to make the dynamic of the song make sense. I think the whole last chorus was a new vocal take." These replacement vocals had again been recorded in David's house, but by this time some longer microphone leads had been acquired so he was able to record in his bedroom while his cohorts were sitting in the living room with the gear – "almost like a proper studio."

Only one edit was required on David's 'Babylon' vocal. "He's a proper singer," said Polson who was apparently not into spending hours chopping up vocals. Because the original vocal was unerasable, the track was muted and the re-recording literally allowed to drown it out.

When East West came on board, more money was available to lavish on 'Babylon' as they prepared for its second outing as a single. "The idea was to make it work on radio," said Polson, explaining that "Those opening moments are always really important. . . you give people something to latch onto so they can recognise the song straight away." The final mix took three days, "blurring all those edges" of the original recording where shortcomings became audible. Real strings could now be used as opposed to the computer-generated kind, though Polson jestingly complained, "It's a lot more difficult working with real people than it is with a computer. They go out of tune and stuff like that." Just tell that to David Gray's guitar! In the end, "We put a lot of effort into the single to give it the best possible chance."

And that would soon pay off. Gray would list the defining moments of cracking his home country as when Capital Radio in London added the twice-revamped 'Babylon' to its 'A' playlist: "That was a big moment, and when Radio 1 added it there, that certainly was a significant thing as far as the success of the record in Britain." Yet he saw the funny side. "It's now more than the record being played, it's as if everyone thinks it's fantastic. Everyone's trumpeting the whole thing and I'm like, 'Hang on, this record came out last year and you didn't say fuck all about it.'"

Media praise came thick and fast. London listings mag *Time Out* compared it favourably to the music of hip Glaswegians The Blue Nile, experts in "rain-splashed melancholia. If there's any justice he'll have a whole new audience now thanks to this warm, romantic record." They praised 'Babylon' as "a hymn of wonderment, its delightful humanity like a sudden burst of sunshine."

The plaudits *White Ladder* received might have been embarrassing for anyone who hadn't had to wait this long for a favourable review. The *Times* rated it "a record that makes your life feel better by its mere existence", while even the hardened weekly 'inkies' gave him the belated thumbs-up. "David Gray is one of pop's enduring Mavericks," insisted *Melody Maker* of a man who played "ear-stinging acoustic guitar, writes songs like beaten brass and sings like Van Morrison dipped in Welsh diphthongs." Style bible *Q* enthused over the new heights hit by "his distinctive emotion-soaked voice, two parts Van Morrison, one part Kevin Coyne." It was all grist to the mill, and a white sticker on the CD case duly carried a selection of press superlatives.

David's first producer Dave Anderson went out and bought his own copy of *White Ladder*. His opinion? "There's obviously a link, he still has that emotional intensity, he's still basically a singer-songwriter singing his songs, though he puts it in a slightly different frame now. Essentially, though, it's the same David Gray."

Did he have any idea his charge would become an international megastar? "Well, obviously I hoped he would (laughs). It's just a shame it took nine years to happen."

CHAPTER 7

America

After the many and various disasters he'd suffered on American soil, from playing support to spare ribs to the runaway tour bus, you couldn't have blamed David Gray for giving up altogether on the idea of Stateside stardom. But his musical heroes were a croaky-voiced American and a US-based Irishman, so he had no intention of throwing in the towel.

Even in 1994, he'd felt he'd have a fairer crack of the whip on the opposite side of the water. "Van Morrison, Bob Dylan, Neil Young, Joni Mitchell, Tom Waits – they've been around for bloody ages, done loads of stuff, but somehow there's a big gap between them and all the people who are trying to get a new thing going with a Nineties kind of angle. . . I mean, American newcomers get treated well, because they're from a mystical culture, like Irish people do as well. There's a mystery to English people about those places – I don't know what the fuck it is, but they're mystified!

"But they've been made into myths, all these people [who've been around]. They failed and messed up as much as anybody did, in their musical careers, and they didn't get to their heights by sheer brilliance: they worked their way up, like, for ages. Now they're these legends, and you step into the shadow of that, people compare you but you're never on the same footing. It's a really stifling situation that we've got all these established figures and people expect you to be up there side by side with them – but they've been there for 30 years..."

The big advantage he had this time round was momentum. The *White Ladder* bandwagon was already rolling, and its appearance on the market for other labels to snap up coincided with South African-born US-based musician Dave Matthews forming his own company. Matthews, who had invited Gray to open the show on tour in 1995 and was a big fan of his first record, *A Century Ends*, thought the singer-songwriter would be a great initial signing for his new label. "I closed my mind to anything else for probably a month after I listened to that record," Matthews said of his first hearing of *White Ladder*. "It was the only record in my car."

East West Records' affiliation with Warner Brothers had given David another option, but, mindful of his EMI America problems, he decided he'd rather be number one in a field of one than repeat the experience of being a major-label minnow. "I mean, there's only a couple of people at the record company," he enthused. "His label is actually like two or three people, so that's an interesting situation. The head of the company was driving us around on the tour and flying around with us from city to city. So, you get hands-on contact. You're the only artist on the roster for one thing, so it's not like if they don't get this record going, they can go and do something else. They are going to have to make it work. That was a major part of why we decided to go with them."

Matthews' own route to the top had been a roundabout one, to say the least, making Gray's physical displacements look small. Born in Johannesburg, South Africa, in 1967, the son of a physicist father who worked for IBM and an architect mother, his family had relocated to New York state when he was just two. Another childhood year was spent in London, but, after his father died from cancer when he was ten, the family returned to Johannesburg. Unwilling to do South African military service at 18, he moved back to the US, settling eventually in Charlottesville, Virginia.

Having formed a band, released a self-financed album and spent three years building a fan base through a schedule of 200 nights a year on the road, Matthews (whose music has been compared with everything from folkies Fairport Convention through Peter Gabriel to Pearl Jam) signed with RCA Records. His first major-label album, 1994's *Under The Table And Dreaming*, went to Number 11 on the strength of their live following. Two years later, *Crash* entered the *Billboard* listings at Number 2, while two years after that *Before These Crowded Streets* went that all-important one place better.

By the end of the Nineties, the Dave Matthews Band were selling out Chicago's 10,000 capacity Soldier Field twice running and packing stadiums from Boston to Los Angeles – feats matched only by the legendary names in popular music. And when 2001's *Everyday*, recorded with Alanis Morissette producer Glen Ballard, attained the Number 1 position, his place at rock's top table was assured.

But Matthews had put in the groundwork, earned the street smarts. Not only had he self-financed a pre-RCA effort, *Remember Two Things*, to sell on the road as a merchandise item, but in 1996, he launched an attack on bootleggers in conjunction with the US Federal Government, targeting stores that were selling illegal discs of his band's live performances. The efforts of Matthews, his band and management resulted in an unprecedented crackdown on bootleggers in early 1997, where nearly all of the major foreign bootlegging companies were arrested by the United States, thereby putting the brake on the entire underground industry.

To further combat the bootleggers, and long before Pearl Jam followed a similar strategy, Matthews released a pair of official concert albums, *Live At Red Rocks 8-15-95* (1997) and *Listener Supported* (1999). The double *Red Rocks* was an unexpected success, debuting at Number 3 on the charts and selling a million copies within the first five months of its release.

Along with the record success came the spin-offs. The DMB's self-owned merchandising company, run out of a specially-built 2000 square foot warehouse slap bang in the Virginia countryside, shipped more than a million Dave Matthews Band T-shirts every year and grossed and estimated annual $80 million, helping Matthews make the listing of the Top 40 biggest earners in showbiz. So while Matthews retained radical and alternative views, he clearly knew the value of a dollar. Certainly, his deal with David was unusual. "They haven't given us an advance or anything," Gray confirmed.

The two Davids had first encountered each other some years earlier in Boulder, Colorado, when the American came up to him and gave him one of his CDs. Both were in town as part of the annual SXSW (South By Southwest) conference of music-business movers and shakers. "That's when I met him first. I'd just done an in-store promo at (local record shop) Albums on the Hill. I don't know how he'd got hold of my record, but he knew all about me and was very into it."

Their paths didn't cross for a couple of years, until they did a few gigs together. Gray: "His career was sort of on the up slope at that particular point; mine was kind of hovering in the dubious netherregions. I didn't really think any more of it, but I watched his career sort of take off: 'Oh wow, look, he's doing well', 'Christ, he's really doing well' and 'Jesus, he's taking over the world!' And then, strangely enough, he's thinking of setting up a label, and I'm thinking how to get our record out in the US, and the two things sort of merged at just the right moment, just when we were about to try some other distribution idea."

Matthews' drolly named According To Our Records (usually abbreviated to ATO) officially signed David Gray early in 2000. He knew Matthews was a big fan of his, and didn't think him "the sort of capricious kind of whimsical pop star who would have a label just to indulge himself. He wants to make it work, and we sensed a genuine spine behind the whole label, having heard all the bullshit in the past." Matthews' opinion of *White Ladder* was a sales pitch in itself. "It's phenomenal, an amazing piece of work. I think of it like (Dylan's) 'Blood On The Tracks', like (Carole King's) 'Tapestry'."

Gray certainly felt Matthews' fast-expanding business organisation was the right outlet at the right time. "All the people who've been involved with the record have had a profound effect upon it. Obviously, there was only so much we could do ourselves, so it's all been working perfectly. There's been no clash; I had to listen to hardly any bullshit about people's opinions, what they think. We had already given them a finished product; it was very satisfying to just get on with the business side of it."

Matthews' operation could make use of the same RCA/BMG distribution network that brought his records to the marketplace. "One of the big problems is that everyone thinks (selling records is) a science," Gray said, "and that's why it's become so incredibly dull. It's been left with businessmen who talk of music in some sort of insane, accountant-style fashion. The whole thing was not founded on sane thought. How can you explain what happened when Elvis picked up a guitar and shook his hips? He lit up an entire world. That's not going to make any sense. You can't have plans for that."

Gray's attachment and attraction to the new world came from classic American songwriting – something he feels is "not a pop craft, there's something more ancient about it. It comes from folk, the mountains, the blues. In *Nebraska*, which I think is Springsteen's best record, you don't need instrumentation, you just need your imagination. These lines come from experience, it's a craft like a blacksmith hammering something out. He's staking everything – the ghost of his father, not having things and always wanting them. Then he got those things and he learnt that they weren't how he wanted them to be. He'd been on the poor side of the tracks. He'd looked at the world, seen it all shining. I feel a massive connection with all that stuff. And now you're in the big shiny world you can't go back to the other one, it's a strange position to be in."

Dave Matthews had originally been persuaded to form a label by friends Michael McDonald (no relation to the same-name singer) and Chris Tetzeli. "They asked me if I wanted to join with them and start up a new record company. And I said, sure. The goals were simple. We wanted to have a bit of control. There are a lot of great musicians out there that don't get anything. And then there's a lot of bad music that gets everything. We wanted to change that."

As for the link with David Gray, he explained to *Acoustic Guitarist* magazine that "I've known him for years and I've listened to all his records. He was looking for a label to release (*White Ladder*) in America and I knew this record was out all over the world, but he couldn't get it released in America, which shows sort of how messed up the industry is. But this is an album that is overflowing with greatness. I find inspiration in David Gray and so therefore I think that other people will find inspiration in David Gray. I think there will always be artists that are going to support other artists because it's the nature of music."

Matthews' basic, grass-roots marketing style was, he confessed, "the only way we know how to do things". As previously mentioned, the first stage of ATO's marketing campaign was sending label president McDonald and vice president Tetzeli across the country on tour with Gray to play *White Ladder* to radio stations. "It must mean something if the president of the record company drives from city to city with it – that's a pretty big endorsement," said the singer. "We thought the record didn't really need anything more than for someone to listen to it. Once somebody's heard it a couple of times, you're in."

Indeed, that's just the way it worked. The video for 'Babylon' was given 'Blowtorch' status on MTV's sister station M2, lighting the way for *White Ladder* to finally see the light of day in America on ATO Records in late March 2000, almost two years after its original Irish release but mere weeks after the ink had dried. Its packaging was different from the original version, now including the printed song lyrics inside its cover. The CD's audio content featured two bonus tracks, 'Nightblindness' (originally the B-side of 'This Year's Love' and already on the revamped UK *White Ladder*) and the re-worked single 'Babylon II', while an enhanced section accessible via a computer featured 12 minutes of visual entertainment. This came in the form of an interview and concert footage of 'Please Forgive Me', one of the highlights of the legendary Point Depot, Dublin concert.

Though more copies of *White Ladder* had been bought by US fans as high-priced imports than *Sell, Sell, Sell* had sold through the shops, David remained very optimistic. "I think with this record, when it gets airplay, it works for itself. We've had a particular radio station in Los Angeles called KCRW and they've been playing it to death. We sold thousands of imports in LA on the strength of that. Things have actually moved along in our absence which is the way we like it. You don't have to do the work!"

Nevertheless, a promotional push would seem the next step, and a mini-tour of America was set up to mark *White Ladder's* belated arrival as a domestic release, including an appearance on NBC-TV's chat show *Late Night with Conan O'Brien*. The jaunt appropriately kicked off with a gig at SXSW (South By Southwest), being staged this particular year in Austin, Texas. Next stop was Boston on St Patrick's Day – much to the delight of the city's Irish contingent, who were already more than familiar with *White Ladder* – and on through Philadelphia, New York (the Bowery Ballroom), LA (the Troubadour, where Elton John and others had showcased on their way up), San Francisco and Seattle. All venues sold out well in advance.

The hit of the tour was Clune, with his spiky wit, distinctive Hawaiian shirts and all-action drum style. David was quick to hail the alternative visual focus of the show while reminding us of his musical attributes. "He's got real feel, he plays the drums like a melodic instrument. You could just listen to him alone, he's that good. We have a real rhythmic understanding, Clune and I. That's the real core of the band and in fact the core of the music. I don't want to leave out the rest of the band, though, they're great."

If David's Irish fans had been just a little on the intense side, he had quickly found out that American-style fan worship could get even more spooky. The first time he toured the States and arrived in Los Angeles he found he had attracted his very first stalker! "I didn't notice him to begin with. Then I was like, 'There's that fucking guy again!' He was a weird little guy, crawled up from the mountains or something. At the end of it, I was lying by the swimming pool with some ridiculous hangover, and he walked in calmly, walked around the swimming pool, and presented me with this photo album, which was basically me doing all the things I'd done in Los Angeles. It was like, 'Here you are buying some Fritos. Here you are buying some potato chips. . .'"

Gray's rapport with American audiences varied. In general terms, he didn't find them that different from elsewhere – "They make this weird whooping noise, 'Whoo, yeah', but apart from that. . ." – and thought it difficult to generalise. "You've got New Orleans, Texas, San Francisco, New York, Boston. . . they're not all the same. There's a different vibe in different cities. Los Angeles, for example, is always a bit of a funny one. The wanker quotient is way too high. There are too many music-business people. They're very laid-back too, where San Francisco is just mad." The gambling/matrimony capital of Las Vegas came in for the most stick. "It's a hideous carbuncle on the face of humanity. It's not my kind of place. My kind of place is a quiet place like the beach with a glass of wine."

He acknowledged that the majority of his US audience would only have heard 'Babylon', and saw his job as reeling them in with the other delights in his locker. "A lot of people are there just because of that song. They heard that song and bought that record or they're curious or whatever. They're not just like leaving after they hear the single. They're getting the music. That's just one song out of nineteen that we play in a night. So, that's a good thing. They're engaging with the whole set."

Another audience-building tactic, of course, was to open for a bigger act, exposing their fans to your music and hoping for a few 'conversions'. With his label boss set to play a stadium tour in the summer of 2000, the obvious connection was made – but no sooner had Dave Matthews offered his protégé opening slots on some of his summer dates than Gray's father was taken ill and he decided to remain in England (though it was a last-minute decision, his presence being advertised for some dates). As for any possible musical collaboration between the two Davids, DG played it cool. "Nothing's planned at present. I'm not much of one for collaborating. I'm terribly backwards with fusing to the music industry."

But American radio had certainly taken to the newcomer, and in retrospect it seems he was the right person at exactly the right time. Bruce Jones, programme director for Salt Lake City's KENZ, believed 'Babylon' was "a relief from the rock guitar sound that was so prevalent in 2000." *White Ladder* was, he believed, "a great album (that) really stands out on the air in a unique way."

David, for his part, favoured the spoken word over the written as a means of getting his point across. "The reason journalism doesn't work most of the time is 'cos the artist isn't there to say, 'No, hang on I didn't say that. . .'. That's why radio interviews are better most of the time, 'cos it's all there to be seen – not just the bits that are chopped out and layered with whatever they wanted it all to mean. Most people have made their minds up before you've spoken to them and they just want you to reaffirm a few things. That's the way it works. . . I'm not saying that what gets written is crap. . . I'm saying that I can't deal with everybody's criticisms."

On 24 March it was time to pay back Los Angeles' KCRW's radio station for their long-time support by appearing on their legendary *Morning Becomes Eclectic*, a show broadcast across the Internet. The worldwide web was certainly helping spread the word about David Gray across the world, though he himself found it most useful for finding out the latest soccer scores concerning his beloved Manchester United. (Gray has shown little sign of becoming a 'web head' and, when asked what his favourite site was in a questionnaire, said he "supposed" he'd have to nominate his own.)

Reports were that David was looking quite tired at the end of the tour, but he felt it had served its purpose. "I think we've got sort of a cult following in some places, almost like we've deprived people of our presence for so long, it's whetted the appetite a bit. The last gigs we did were in New York in '97, but really the last tour was in '96. That was in our own right, actually. It was a miserable failure! We failed because then we realised we definitely weren't a great rock act. Get the samplers out!"

If the liaison with the Dave Matthews Band was proving a profitable one for David Gray, it had caused more controversy among his fans than almost anything. Fine if you liked both acts, but merely because Matthews dug Gray it was no guarantee his fans would – nor that the feeling would be reciprocated. The DMB was memorably described by one Gray bulletin-board poster as "sophisticated rock for the Starbucks (coffee house) crowd," adding that "Just because you can compose a song that runs longer than six or seven minutes, that doesn't make you talented. Signing David Gray to his label does not under any circumstances indicate that Dave Matthews himself has talent. All it shows is that he recognises a good thing when he sees it. So do I. And I crack windows when I sing." Perhaps the last word on this one should reside with David Gray: "Whatever you think of Dave Matthews, he is not full of shit."

Certainly, Matthews had snagged David Gray at a point when the US airwaves were slowly opening to an act of his vintage and values. There had been a rash of female singer/songwriters on the late-Nineties charts, the likes of Alanis Morissette and the Sheryl Crow/Lilith Fair branch of performers, while the leading male singer/songwriters had tended to form rock bands around themselves. Lilith founder Sarah McLachlan conceded that "There were great male singer/songwriters like David Gray and Ron Sexsmith who couldn't get played on the radio a few years ago if it killed them. At one point, there were certain stations that played nothing but women. It was like, 'Women are hot, so we're not going to bother with men.' I just wish there was more of a sense of balance."

And that balance was restored courtesy of a backlash against some female singer/songwriters who came to the fore in the Lilith era. "When the last Jewel album came out, there was only one hit," said Sean Ross, editor of radio magazine *Airplay Monitor*. "The last Alanis Morissette album didn't have many hits, either." He pointed to the cyclical nature of pop charts and playlists. "Eventually, radio turns on anything that it plays a lot of," he says. "I guess the cycle turns on what (programmers) get sick of."

Once the female dominance had ended, however, the pendulum swung too far over, making acts like Limp Bizkit and Linkin Park – in McLachlan's words, "bands making that kind of harder, slightly misogynistic music" – the first beneficiaries. But Gray was able to find his constituency in the middle ground, thanks to supporters in the media like MTV's Bill Flanagan, the man behind the cable channel's *Storytellers* segment, who identified Gray as a "great, classic singer/songwriter." Americans John Hiatt and Don Henley, the ex-Eagle, were also both fans, albeit from an older generation of writer/performer who were themselves suffering from a generational split that has affected some older rock artists. In Sean Ross's view, this was because US radio was now populated by "26-year-old programme directors who don't want to play Billy Joel."

And it was interesting to reflect that the other British artist climbing the US charts at speed, Dido, also used modern technology to spice up her music. "I think songwriting has to move into the next century," said David to the publication *USA Today*, reasoning that he had to use any means possible to evade the "huge shadows" cast by "massive characters in the singer/songwriter field that have. . . been a bit daunting for those coming after them. But maybe there's enough of a gap now that it can be done differently."

At last, David Gray was not only a star, he was revelling in it. "I had become so well-versed in my own insecurity, but what's been amazing over the last year and a half is watching all that fall away," he says, "letting go of that agenda of blame – you know, the world's fucked up, the record company's wankers. All that negativity. When you do something right – when you just let something happen, and you're doing it with every pore of your being – good things happen. And I can't help but think that's one reason people respond to this record: the story is real."

CHAPTER 8

America Succumbs

Having done America the hard way a few short years previously, David Gray would be back in the Big Apple in July 2000 ready to reach out to millions through the medium of television. It was certainly a lot easier that trekking up and down the Midwest playing second billing to menus.

Needless to say, the backstage hospitality on the *Late Night With David Letterman* chat show (the prestigious equivalent of Britain's *Parkinson*) was not only more expansive but considerably more cultured. 'Babylon' was delivered in suitably professional fashion by the man and his band as he contemplated a rather more upmarket US tour than the ones he'd played three years earlier. Truly, this was a triumphant return for a man who had once been an untouchable – now any number of US labels would gladly have killed for his signature.

Not that every gig he'd play would be a huge one. Schuba's in Chicago, a tavern holding around 300 fans, was sold out long before the late-March show.* Those who attended knew the words of each

---

* The venue was a semi-legendary one; keen-eyed movie-goers may recall a poster advertising the unlikely-named Ladyboy Transistor gracing the pad of John Cusack's record-shop owner in the film version of Nick Hornby's *High Fidelity*. The fact the book had set the action in London is neither here nor there.

song and sang them with gusto, at such deafening volume that Gray halted his own singing on a number of occasions and listened to them with a smile. The set list had code names for every song played, to keep the sense of fun. (To add to the light-hearted mood, Gray had taken to registering in hotels under the name of Cheeky Monkey.) At one point the band had played a short riff between songs, causing a chuckling Gray to comment, "So, *that's* (the song) 'Hairpiece'!"

The sardine-packed crowd may not have understood the joke, but the music had certainly made the right connections. Schuba's was so compact it didn't even have a dressing room, so Clune hid behind his drums as the others crouched down on their haunches in an attempt to 'disappear' from the watching eyes of the crowd which clapped, sang, stomped and whistled them back into view. It was certain their return to Chicago would be somewhere far grander – even if more than a little of the intimacy would have to be sacrificed.

If it was the beginning of a new life for *White Ladder*, the phenomenon was far from a spent force at home. The album was passing over the counter at a rapid rate, 30,000 copies a week by the record company's reckoning, and David's new-found public awaited. So, strange though it was to be promoting two-year-old recordings as the world caught up, he was given just on night in his London home to sleep off the jet-lag before being chauffeured to a helicopter landing pad. Next stop the *Radio 1 Roadshow*!

The gathering at Moss Bank Park in Bolton had the biggest audience of the *Roadshow* tour so far with 80,000 people turning up for a mixed bill of pop and dance acts. David was to play just one song there before 'coptering back to London for an appearance at the Guildford Festival in front of a 'mere' 30,000 souls. He was ten minutes late on stage – understandable, in the circumstances – and surprisingly low down the pecking order behind Jools Holland, Joan Armatrading and his hero, Van Morrison. The mid-afternoon spot reflected the fact that he had been booked some time before the success of *White Ladder*, but the packed field in front of the main stage was a far better barometer of his current popularity.

Hiccups on the day included bassist Rob Malone going absent without leave just before the signal to take the stage and a stuttering keyboard – "technology!" Gray good-naturedly cursed – but once

'Babylon' had elicited the loudest cheers of the afternoon so far David and company were home free. Clune hurled his drum sticks across the stage in triumph as they finished.

Maybe it was jet-lag, but he seemed to take the past days' jetsetting in his stride. "It's a bit scary when you first take off, you're like 'Hello, we're in a small glass bubble flying through the air'. Had a helicopter, then a police escort, so that's a first – just after breakfast, that's how I like to start my day! It's a completely ridiculous life."

That life became even more ridiculous when, just eight days after his last US show in Boston, he found himself hanging round the set of *TFI Friday*, the cult television programme hosted by scenemaker Chris Evans. The link was one born out of mild desperation – you scratch my back, I'll scratch yours. The DJ turned media millionaire, whose Ginger Productions had bought and would sell Virgin Radio for a tidy profit, found his ratings for the Channel 4 show were slipping, so had decided to transmit the late-night edition live, bringing in some high-profile guests to boost the must-watch factor (and Shaun Ryder for the possibility of live on-air swearing). For David's record label, the album had risen on the chart again to Number 13 and, with the re-release of 'Babylon' pending, all the promotional muscle of the company was being flexed in an attempt to breach the Top 10 in both formats.

Hence the hours before the show found our man sorting through clothes purchased that very afternoon by the record company's stylist. Aside from dressing up in relatively flamboyant garb, the experience wasn't one he seemed to savour. "It's when you actually have to sing that it's sort of grotesque," he told *Hot Press* magazine's ever-attentive reporter. "Having to be soul-baring in the most unlikely and unconducive scenarios gets on my wick. I'm obviously going to be in for an onslaught of inane situations, and I think it's best to try to enjoy it. If I fight it, I'll just drive myself crazy." David went on, played 'Babylon', then got on with the rest of his life. Quite how he managed to deliver the too-familiar words with the same vitality must be wondered at.

The other guests on the show included a near namesake, Scots soccer pundit Andy Gray, and Irish sisters The Corrs. Sharon and Andrea were fans, just like the majority of their country-people, and even took the time to say so. "I think he's the Neil Young of our era," said

Sharon. "Last night at two o'clock in the morning, I couldn't get to sleep and I was listening to that album (*White Ladder*). I just kept rewinding and listening to it again, so I suppose you could say he's better than sleep!" Andrea agreed with the back-handed compliment. "I think the songs are fantastic. They're very true, very honest, and it's music for music's sake, which is rare these days."

As well as television, the Internet was spreading the word about David Gray – and a proliferation of sites would sprout like mushrooms in the post-*White Ladder* period. Millennium hangovers had only just begun to subside when, in January 2000, the doors of the Pink Flamingo Lounge opened for business. One of the most professionally styled and run Gray websites, it attracted 500 hits in its first week on-line.

There was no doubt that the Internet suited David Gray's intense core following of Grayites down to the ground. Silver Lining, run by fan Derek Figg, was the most established of the DG sites (and the first to put up MP3s of live music) but was to be surpassed by both The Pink Flamingo Lounge and Drunken Gibberish. Maybe he ran into problems with the MP3s or, as seems to have happened with others, the webmaster/mistress lost interest once 'their' artist became public property. However, Shine, Living Room and New Horizons deserve credit for being pioneers.

The obligatory www.davidgray.com came into its own once 'Babylon' became a hit, but with little input from the man himself. It remained the province of the 'Grayites' to produce the best web work. Trying To Make Sense Of The Rain, David Gray Heaven and Sorrowful Moon were among the newer arrivals, the latter two concentrating on making guitar tablature and lyrics of his music – even the unreleased songs – available to all who wanted them.

Meanwhile the Internet had helped Gray-mania hit Australia when a music store called Choppers founded a website, www.go.to/white-ladder, in September 2000 and received an amazing 1400 hits in just 10 days from music lovers all over the world.

The website included song lyrics, biography, photos and Australian press reviews and interviews. "It might seem strange that we've chosen to create a website for an international artist," said store owner Pat Smith, "but as soon as we heard this album we knew it was something special. It has really taken off in the UK and Ireland and we think the same will happen here if we can help spread the word."

Choppers' efforts to single-handedly champion the Gray cause to the entire Northern Rivers area included hiring out the shop next door to create a giant display. As a result, 'Babylon' was added to the playlists of local radio stations as far away as Perth. According to Narelle Smith, Pat's wife and co-owner, "We're determined to introduce as many people as possible to David Gray. We're going to break this artist Australia-wide out of Lismore!"

Gray himself remained charmingly cautious as to the potential of the worldwide web, and the fact his fans seemed to have plugged into it with a vengeance. "I suppose I'm asking for it, really, with my heart-on-sleeve style," he admitted, but revealed that dialling into his own website message board had shocked him. "It gets a bit crazy at times. They don't have enough of a grip on real life, like this is so important. It's unbelievable how they really fight and scruple about things: 'He's a sell-out 'cause he's doing this.' 'He's not selling out. He should be doing that.' 'He's selling out.' 'He's not selling out. . .' You can't actually listen to it. It's just some ridiculous dialogue."

In some ways, he felt it a back-handed tribute to his own powers of communication. "Because my songs are kind of wordy and they're quite revealing and they're open – the emotions in them – people think they know me because they've listened to the music and it meant something to them." As for the Internet in general, "I'm unconvinced, but I can see it's incredible and the immediacy with which you can communicate. I like the e-mail vibe, but it seems that the whole thing is turning into a grotesque commercial show."

Talking of things commercial, EMI Ireland re-released *Sell, Sell, Sell* on 7 July 2000, just as the new *Lost Songs* débuted at Number 1 in the Irish charts and *White Ladder*, boosted by the singles success of 'Babylon', climbed to Number 2 on the UK album chart. It wasn't a situation that pleased David overmuch, and he clearly considered his late unlamented label was cashing in on his current success. "Record companies are cynical bastards," he reflected, "But they've got to make their money back. . . let's get it out before (success) disappears again."

His main complaint, however, was that EMI's reissue might make people buy the wrong record. He told Radio 1: "I don't think they've made it clear enough that it's a record made five or six years ago. Everybody smells blood because success has come and they're all thinking let's make some of the money back we spent on him," he shrugged. "There's nothing really I can do about it. There's things I'm not so happy about but there's nothing I can do about it. I'm best concentrating on what I'm doing now, which is what's causing all this."

In another bout of music-business Monopoly, EMI had taken over Virgin/Hut when Richard Branson had sold them to raise more money to run his airline. Having the rights to David's first three long-players, they had considered issuing a double *Best Of* album of pre-*White Ladder* material which, it was rumoured, would include no fewer than 15 unreleased tracks. David himself was underwhelmed – "It's a bit early for archiving my life, in my opinion; maybe in ten years' time" – but it confirmed that his behind-the-scenes efforts to reclaim the rights to his earlier albums from Virgin and EMI had proved unsuccessful; predictably enough, given his recent commercial success.

White Ladder had been revamped with a cover slightly different from the original, and the single B-side, 'Nightblindness', as track five. It still contained the secret opening track but not the enhanced elements of the American release. Happily for fans, the lyrics had now been included in the insert – unhappily for the myopic, presented as one long sentence! The re-released 'Babylon' had similarly been accorded a new video, directed by Mike Figgis (of *Leaving Las Vegas* fame) and shot in London's Paddington underground station.

The summer of 2000 saw David Gray media saturation. *White Ladder* found release in August in Australia, where EastWest mounted a large scale campaign similar to that run in the UK (undoubtedly boosted by the efforts of Choppers website!). David hosted MTV2 on August 7, underlining his presence on the cover of almost every music magazine in Britain and Ireland, not to mention magazines, newspapers and the Internet.

Having been voted best non-Irish artist in '99, David cleaned up at the annual *Hot Press* Readers' Poll 2000. His seven victories in the International section included best male singer, best single ('Please Forgive Me'), best album and best songwriter.

More had, meanwhile, surfaced about the origins of bassist Rob

Malone, who in February 2000 could be found in Dublin playing with the Hothouse Flowers who had re-formed to played a one-off charity gig at the Tivoli. Rob was a veteran of Drive-By Truckers, a supposed psychobilly or country-punk-rock band (take your pick) formed in 1996 in R.E.M.'s home town of Athens, Georgia, though their debut release Gangstabilly, which included tracks entitled 'Wife Beater', 'The Living Bubba', 'Steve McQueen' and 'Buttholeville', had been recorded before his arrival. He played a full part in second album, 'Pizza Deliverance', hailed as "an exercise in Southern gothic at its finest. . . the humour and tragedy of life in the south are portrayed with all the naked (sur)realism of the finest velvet-Elvis you've ever witnessed." Song titles on the album, appearing on the band's own Soul Dump label, included 'Bulldozers And Dirt', 'Nine Bullets', 'The President's Penis' and 'The Night GG Allen Came To Town.'

Supernumerary pedal steel player John Neff augmented the four-piece though "the sweet sounds of the pedal steel can't mask the simmering sleaze underneath". The lewd and beautiful lyrics came courtesy of primary singer/songwriter Patterson Hood, son of famed Muscle Shoals bass player Roger Hood.

Mike Cooley extolled his colleague's commitment. "He switched to bass (from guitar) and was willing to play it indefinitely. He never questioned it; he just made it work. That's what it takes." By the time of the live *Alabama Ass Whuppin'* (1999), Malone had returned to guitar to cement a Lynyrd Skynyrd three-axe line-up, his bass place being taken by sound technician Earl Hicks. Then came the call from David Gray – but don't rule out the possibility of 'Buttholeville' or 'The President's Penis' turning up as an unscheduled encore sometime.

Late June had seen Gray make a triumphant return to Glastonbury. While the previous year had seen him quite reasonably sited in the New Bands Tent, June 2000 saw Gray gracing an altogether larger stage. A slot on a side (Other) stage had already been secured, but when master American songsmith Burt Bacharach pulled out at short notice, the vacant main (Pyramid) stage spot was offered. The special guest performance was therefore foreshortened so that David could extend his Sunday set. He learned of the situation when Radio 1 caught up with him. "You know more about it than I do!" he chortled into the proffered microphone, but emphasised that "it's a big deal to me that we'll be on the main stage. If we've got an extra long set that's an extra big deal."

And the result was a predictable triumph. Opening with 'Sail Away', he was clearly preaching to the converted: a head count of *White Ladder* owners would doubtless have elicited a sea of hands. He was, dotmusic website's reviewer concluded, "The perfect sound for a sunny afternoon in the open air," and even though the grey clouds were rolling in as he ended the set with 'Please Forgive Me' he left the customers satisfied.

But Oliver Gray ("no relation, unfortunately", as he qualified his by-line in the festival newspaper) caught both shows and was able to reveal some clever tactical set-reshaping that had gone on between the two appearances. "The Saturday slot on the Other Stage showed the band demonstrating its clever gift for mixing their folk-rooted songs with dance-tinged beats," he wrote, "and when David filled in for Burt Bacharach (some coup) it was crucial the momentum built up the previous day should be maintained.

"Proceedings weren't easy, since a largely acoustic set of probably unfamiliar to most songs had to compete with following Jools Holland, not to mention a passing ear-splitting carnival procession. But David Gray is a pro. Not only did he play an entirely different set but he also slowed down proceedings dramatically compared to the previous day and risked concluding with a brand new song. The crazy echo-fest with which they climaxed their Pyramid performance was the nearest this year's festival will get to Led Zeppelin."

The biggest thrill for Gray, though, had been meeting David Bowie – a man whose numerous career reinventions made *White Ladder* look pretty tame. "The day we played the main stage at the Glastonbury Festival was the day that the single ('Babylon') went in at Number 5 on the British charts," he said. "We also met David, and were having a chat with him. Plus all our family and friends were there. That was amazing. It took about a week to calm down, if in fact I did."

Gray's favourite Bowie album had been *Hunky Dory*, his singer-songwriter opus from 1972 that had preceded the Ziggy Stardust phase. "This was a brilliant record. Think of his records and how different they all were. How was he going to keep that up? His vibe was getting the right people involved; he was a genius for getting a new sound or a new direction. He was the best.

"For me, Bowie *was* pop music: he had his moment. I listened to all his records and would get dead excited because he's an enigma. He was in a rock band, and before that he was a folkie. Within 10 years he'd covered the lot. I loved him."

Gray's omnipresence at the festivals this summer was on a par with that of Travis in 1999, and, just as they'd crested a commercial wave with *The Man Who*, *White Ladder* would enjoy similar success through the summer – winning Top 5 status, as David had remarked, in Glastonbury week. The album had first nudged into a UK chart dominated by long-stayers in Moby, Tom Jones and Santana on 13 May, providing Top 20 resident Macy Gray with a bit of healthy sibling rivalry. It rose in the ranks from 69 through 44 to 32, satisfyingly overtaking the soundtrack to the year's film phenomenon, *Gladiator*.

Next came the jump into the 30, Number 23 being one place higher than soul sister Macy. Onwards and upwards it forged, symbolically swapping places with *The Man Who* en route to Number 13 in mid June. Its momentum appeared to have dissipated as it paused for breath, but the first chart of July saw a sudden spurt to Number 8. The top spot might be ruled by Eminem, but a blow for real music was clearly being struck by the silent majority. Astoundingly, the Top 5 was its next destination, hitting first 4 and then 2 behind the crew-cutted rapper in mid July.

The straight-in entry of Coldplay with the outstanding *Parachutes* ensured the top spot would remain tantalisingly out of reach, but the end of July saw *White Ladder* still in the Top 5 and exchanging its gold symbol (100,000 sales) for a platinum marker (300,000). It would remain in the Top 5 till the last week of August, buoyed both by the festival shows and the success of the reissued 'Babylon'.

Late September brought another surge upwards to Number 4, while a further month in the Top 10 brought double platinum certification. Not until mid November 2000 would *White Ladder* lose its grip on a Top 10 rung. And that, as we'll see, was far from the end of that particular story.

CHAPTER 9

Lost Songs and Awards

Two days of post–Glastonbury rehearsals had preceded a brace of capital gigs at Shepherds Bush Empire, the original 3 August date selling out (hardly surprising, with tickets a more than reasonable £12.50) and the ever-willing David adding a show the previous night.

Previewing the event, Q magazine suggested that word of mouth would ensure a sell-out crowd. "As with all the best singer-songwriters, once people lock into Gray's polished folk-rock, they become committed disciples, keen to convert their friends. So expect every song to be greeted with rapturous devotion – especially the one that doesn't belong to him, as the now trademark saunter through Soft Cell's 'Say Hello, Wave Goodbye' is always a high-point." It's amazing how many critics have highlighted the one non-original from *White Ladder* as a reference point. . .

Next came a familiar experience: the flight to Ireland, where he was to play Witnness – a two-day Festival rather than any form of religious conversion. He appeared on the August bank holiday to headline the first day of the biggest festival in Ireland that summer, held at the Firhouse race track and sponsored by the national drink, Guinness. The festival featured over 50 live acts across five stages over the two days, including such famous names as Beck, Travis and Ocean Colour Scene. This event would dwarf the Point Depot (8,000) and even his support gig at Slane '99 in David's personal league table of people played to, while his headlining status was testament to his popularity and attraction in Ireland.

"I didn't realise the power of it all," he confessed to *Select* magazine a few weeks afterwards, "but (at the Witness festival) the penny dropped. People were going mental and it blew me away. I'm normally quite pragmatic, but I couldn't find a section of my mind to file it in. File under Gig? Sorry, does not compute, not enough RAM. I put it under Insane Experiences."

Critics would compare the moment to Pulp at Glastonbury in 1995, Oasis at Knebworth or the Stone Roses at Spike Island. This was David Gray's moment, the payback for five years' hard work serenading a nation. As the sun set and the funfair lights twinkled in time, artist and a word-perfect audience appeared as one. And the roar at the end of each number sent any number of wild birds soaring to the heavens in alarm – or was it celebration?

Gray called the experience "life-changing". A couple of thousand people in a club was something he'd become accustomed to, "but this was something else. You can't make sense of 40,000 people going nuts." The crowd were indeed delirious – the more so when their hero confessed the adulation was "fucking blowing my mind. . . this is ridiculous."

More adulation was in evidence later in the year at the *Q* Awards, where he received the reader-voted award for 2000's best single in 'Babylon'. (Other candidates had included Coldplay's 'Yellow' and 'The Real Slim Shady' by Eminem, so there was some form of revenge for those acts eclipsing his own album-chart success.) Having totally failed to rise to the occasion, sartorially speaking, in an oversized blue pinstripe shirt (un-tucked in!), he accepted the golden statuette with the following speech: "Erm, weird. This year just keeps getting weirder. What can I say? I don't think there's any such thing as a single of the year, but thanks to everyone who voted anyway."

David had skipped across the Atlantic in August for a US tour, set to officially kick off on the 29th at Washington DC's 9:30 Club and continue through the end of September. Highlight was the Roseland

Ballroom – a favourite of visiting English indie bands like Travis – where he overcame the twin problems of the old-fashioned venue's trademark poor acoustics and an unsuitable opening act, Five For Fighting, to captivate a crowd already note-perfect on the 'White Ladder' material. It was, as Gray noted toward the end of the show, a far cry from the industry showcases held downtown at the Mercury Lounge back in the days when his career was dying a death due to record-company incompetence.

The irony, one reviewer observed, was that "Gray really hasn't got much better than he was earlier in his career – he remains a fantastic performer who's completely consumed by his own music, and it shows. The difference is that people are finally paying attention." The man himself pronounced the mini-tour here "really great, especially the Avalon in Boston. Some good venues and the crowds were brilliant."

October 2000 was to see David's UK tour kick off in what would have been familiar surroundings for him, at Liverpool University on 6 October, and winding up at Wolverhampton Civic Hall on the 23rd of the month. A London date at Brixton had been penned in for 16 December. But the later dates had to be pulled due to illness – hardly surprising after the gruelling schedule he'd undergone during the last few months. Official sources said the singer had "got severe flu and as a result has lost his voice", though it seems he was unwilling to let people down – the Glasgow Barrowlands show was cancelled on the actual day. The dates were rescheduled for the December post-Brixton/pre-Christmas period.

His home-town gig of Manchester in October was acclaimed as the best of the tour, largely because "people here have a bit of attitude. It's always been a tough town to play. Tonight, though, they were the opposite." The larger proportion of those at the Academy probably arrived thinking they were about to witness an Irish singer rather than someone born in suburban Sale, who passionately supported the local football team. They'd be put right on both counts during the course of an entertaining evening.

Indeed he had the audience eating out of his hand as the dance-rock capital of Britain got down to the sounds of one of their own. "It's quite bizarre, isn't it?" he remarked about the split in his audience between those attracted by the singer-songwriter side and those turned on by samplers and machines. "There've always been people at the gigs from the Sixties and Seventies who understand the Dylan-influenced side of it, but then there's this whole other generation – a lot of young women standing side by side with schoolteachers, who probably teach them."

Anyone who'd missed out on a ticket had the consolation of the video of his legendary Point gig from a year previously, released on November 10. A DVD of the gig would follow in February 2001 that combined his 17-song set available on the video with a documentary, *Up To A Point*. *Record Buyer* magazine's review suggested that "though this is no *Bringing It All Back Home*," referring to the DA Pennebaker Dylan documentary, "it is a snapshot in time that will grow in importance as Gray becomes an ever bigger star – as I am certain he will. The logically-titled documentary film charts his progress on the tour that preceded it, and it's fascinating to see those who championed him on radio and in the press trying to explain how he's tapped into a nation's psyche so effectively. The live show includes eight of the ten songs on breakthrough album *White Ladder*."

Interestingly, early journalistic convert Colin Harper who reviewed the video for *Record Collector* magazine, drew parallels with Tony Palmer's *Farewell Cream* documentary from the late Sixties, "while the cutaways of atmospherically washed-out, fixed-camera B&W is redolent of the Hendrix *Band Of Gypsies* film, shot exactly thirty years to the day before. But these are mere teasing effects, for unlike those imperfect documents this film allows the performance to breathe, combining the performer/listener intimacy so essential to Gray's music with a sense of the show's epic scale and the very triumph of old-fashioned integrity over the suffocating machine of the modern music industry that Gray's elevation to stardom represents.

"This multi-camera video, boasting splendid, honest sound mixing, is the record of those performances, roving through the opener, 'Sail Away', through close-ups of Gray and his band. . . In short: sixteen items of brilliance from four albums, plus the stunning 'Flame Turns Blue' from the recent Irish-only CD *Lost Songs 95–98* and a revealing interview appendage make this a heart-warming purchase for those who believe in the power of song."

The year 2000 ended with not one but two triumphant nights at the Brixton Academy in London – the hippest venue in town (Madonna was to visit shortly thereafter, with *A Century Ends* percussionist Steve Sidelnyk in her band). Naturally a sell out at a modest ticket price of £16, the first date on the 16th was webcast by wembleytv.com, while the evening's version of 'This Year's Love' would be released as a CD track early in the new year.

Q magazine previewed the gig as being by "the year's most bizarre success story," remarking sagely that "12 months ago he'd have been happy with the Bull & Gate in Kentish Town." Still, they got it right that "His 12 months of good fortune will give these days a celebratory feel, offering all the feelgood, heart-warming sentiment you'd expect," though they rather spoilt it with the coda, "This should more than compensate for the earnest troubadour routine being dwarfed by such a large venue."

Reviewing for *Uncut* magazine, Nigel Williamson certainly fell under the man's spell. "In 20 years' time," he concluded, "we're all going to be shaking our greying heads and complaining they just don't make them like David Gray any more." Certainly, two hours passed as if as many minutes as the master storyteller weaved his magic. Past gems like 'Everytime' and 'Late Night Radio' were politely received, though the most fervent acknowledgement was obviously reserved for *White Ladder* material.

Uncut's Williamson spotlighted the new 'The Longest Time' as a potential hit single of the future, commenting that he is part if a troubadour tradition that is both timeless and constantly able to renew and refresh itself. "Passionate, committed and romantic," he concluded, "when he raises his voice he cannot help but pour out his heart."

Not that the singer was in the mood to recognise that. "I've had enough of this melodic, mellow crap," he declaimed, a knowing sneer on his face, as he prepared to launch into the first of the evening's two encores. The fact that it was the imminent single 'Please Forgive Me' brought a smile, and also underlined the record label owner's role he'd come to call his own. Rule number one: plug the product!

Background projections of cloud and seascapes somewhat literally accompanied album tracks 'Silver Lining' and 'Sail Away' respectively, while 'This Year's Love', in the words of one amused reviewer, "causes couples throughout the packed auditorium to shoot each other meaningful glances as Gray presides over the scene like some kind of acoustic guitar–wielding cupid."

The same reviewer was animated by "the arrival on stage of a chunky, distinctly Victorian-era looking bra from the direction of one of the more excitable sections of the crowd". But by the time 'Babylon' arrived, the auditorium now "a sea of flailing arms and serenading couples," even he was converted. A cheesy seasonal medley of Mud and Slade's Christmas classics from the Seventies added a humorous postscript.

As previously reported, the next single would be 'This Year's Love' on 19 February, though given the length of time between the film that had titled it and its release, even Gray himself, not to mention long-time fans, must have been somewhat tired of it. It had been rumoured on the Internet that he had returned to the studio before Christmas to record a shorter version of 'Sail Away' for single release, but this was sent down the pecking order to appear, half a year later, in July 2001.

In another celluloid tie-in, his performances of 'Say Hello, Wave Goodbye' and 'Falling Free' were slated to appear on the soundtrack for upcoming film *Our Burden Is Light,* 'a modern love story' starring Jack Rooney, Nathan Webb and Denise Coates. It wasn't hard to see why David's unique talent for combining narrative lyrics with moody splashes of melody appealed so much to film-makers, and it seemed only a matter of time before he extended his *This Year's Love* experience to scoring a whole movie.

The start of any year is the season for awards ceremonies, and as 2001 it was David's turn to find his name in the frame at the Brits. His nomination was deserved, of that there was no question, but the fact he was nominated not for *White Ladder* but *Lost Songs 95–98*, an out-takes collection released in Ireland and not yet due for British consumption The reason was that Brit nominations are dependent on releases appearing in a strictly controlled time period, which *White Ladder* fell outside. Too much time had elapsed since its original release to make it eligible, but the organisers 'cheated' – not that anyone was heard to complain.

David had recently won two categories at the Meteor Irish Music Awards. The first was the best-selling album in Ireland by a male artist, won for *White Ladder*, the second was for Best International Songwriter. This saw him beat Thom Yorke of Radiohead, to whom he'd played support a seeming lifetime ago in 1995. Not that this was on his mind when he received the award. "You know, I had a dream last night that it was 2010," David told an enraptured audience "and *White Ladder* was still in the Top 10. Hopefully it was a nightmare!"

Back at the Brits, the big news was about another singer–songwriter named David – garage star Craig David. The Southampton-born teenager had had been nominated in six categories, including head-to-heads with David in Best British Album and Best Male. But *The Sun* newspaper broke the sensational front-page news two days before the event that David (Craig, that is) was to end up empty-handed. His all-round talent had worked against him, the votes having been spread too thinly

Craig David correctly put his money on Coldplay's *Parachutes*, "a brilliant album", to take an award. When it came to the Best Male, he cannily split his stake between two horses. "David Gray is great, and Robbie Williams has had a really good year so I think they're both in with a good chance of winning." The voting was never going to see the headliner of Slane Castle deposed by his one-time supporting act, but it was an experience to remember for David Gray.

A few short months later, both duelling Davids would come up trumps at the 46th Ivor Novello Awards, held at the Grovenor House Hotel in London's Park Lane on 24 May. Craig David took away three of the top awards: Best Contemporary Song , the Ivors Dance Award and Songwriter of The Year. The 'other' David was happy enough to have written the Best Song Musically And Lyrically (inevitably, 'Babylon').

The Ivors are recognised as the top awards ceremony for British songwriting, the winners chosen by music industry figures from the British Academy of Composers and Songwriters, so it was an occasion to savour. For the record, the songs 'Babylon' beat were 'Trouble' (Coldplay) and 'Never Had A Dream Come True' (S Club 7), while

'Please Forgive Me' had been shortlisted for Best Contemporary Song alongside U2's 'Beautiful Day'.

The success of *White Ladder* had left David Gray with no time to consider his next recorded move. For EastWest, he was effectively a début artist, his previous long-players having been placed elsewhere – and though EMI's reactivated *Sell, Sell, Sell* was doing well at mid price in the wake of his breakthrough, his first two Hut releases remained resolutely out of print.

Yet David Gray had a shot in his locker that could satisfy the demand for new music, while costing him little in terms of time, effort and creative endeavour. In the words of *Blue Peter*, he had several he'd made earlier. This was *Lost Songs 95–98*, the album the Brits had tried to honour.

The interpretation of *Lost Songs* was deliberately ambiguous. They could have been songs David had mislaid, then found again, songs that had remained in the shadow of *White Ladder* or songs he had written while in a state of confusion. What was certain was that a number of songs that had made it as far as the stage act had been shelved when *White Ladder* had come together, being considered part of his 'solo singer-songwriter' past rather than his dance-pop future.

The songs may have dated from the years 1995–98 stated in the title, but the recordings on this album – whose original working title had been *Available Light* and was described by the man himself as "The acoustic album I've been threatening to make for the last few years, arriving a little late" – came together in a ten-day period in October 1999. That, of course, was nine months before 'Babylon' worked its magic and lit the blue touch paper on his career.

He didn't want these songs to go to waste, or conversely be issued as a collection of home recordings and demos. "I had a lot of sparse, kind of melancholy stuff hanging around," he elaborated, concluding "It's a record I perhaps should have made earlier in my career, just me and the acoustic guitar. But because of the turmoil of my career at that time, there was never a record made. And I doubt that anyone would have wanted to make a 'me and a guitar' record anyway." The "live in the studio, no overdubs, very back-to-basics record" had come together at Protocol Studios in the last week of October 1999. The album was finished to a tight schedule, the day before Gray went on tour. He'd given himself the nigh-on impossible schedule of 10 days to record and mix – "and we did it." Gray was credited with 'voice, guitar and Wurlitzer (piano)', Clune with drums, voice and bass. The pair stared out from the back cover of the attractively monochrome booklet, the picture – the only one featuring a supporting musician – underlining their creative partnership. Tim Bradshaw also undertook bass duties (this before Rob Malone's permanent recruitment), as well as handling conventional piano, Wurlitzer and Hammond organ. As was by now the custom, Iestyn Polson engineered and co-produced with Gray and Clune.

The album was originally going to be an Internet-only release both to streamline the record-company workload and emphasise that this wasn't a *White Ladder*, but merely a one-off acoustic album. It would not only educate the newcomers in the style with which David had begun his career but was also a way of thanking longer-term fans for their support. "It's a nice stocking filler for fans who've been on board for the long haul," Gray said. "It'll keep 'em going through the long winter months until our next real record."

It was as much an historical document than a new album, then, and Gray had revealed that, though it would be released in Ireland "for sure. . . whether it comes out in the States is another issue. It's five or six songs that are just me and the guitar, and then four or five with the band. It was really a very simple record. It was more like an archive thing. That wasn't really a creative, getting things off your chest kind thing. That was more a bit of songwriter's house-work."

Having decided to "tidy his cupboard", Gray's criterion for choosing which songs to revisit was a simple one – whatever worked out best in the studio. He went in with about 16 or 17 songs, half a dozen of which failed to make the cut. Possibly more: "There's probably another album like that, that might be able to be made, but, to be honest, that time has passed." Either the song was laid down with vocal and guitar, or the band went for live takes, vocals and all. "I wanted a kind of moment in time, a more old-style recording tech-nique. Just a bit of performance really, to focus the whole thing." The result was "a very subtle, simple acoustic record."

While they decided what they were going to do with it, an idea was mooted for an unusual film project "where we plan to get some people to make films for each track and make a kind of installation out of it." If that was David Gray the art student poking his head above the parapet, it was swiftly withdrawn as the stresses of promoting *White Ladder* in Britain and the States rendered anything but a low-key release for *Songs* unlikely.

The gap years in which these songs came together were of course those between *Sell, Sell, Sell* and *White Ladder* and the sentiments contained therein are suitably soul-searchingly doomy. The connection with Springsteen's similarly sparse *Nebraska* can't be overlooked. Just over thirty minutes long this was an exercise in maudlin melancholy that fell well short of *White Ladder*, harking back instead to the early pair of albums. Air and Jurassic 5 may have been on the home stereo during the making of *White Ladder*, but *Lost Songs* seemed to draw from the directness of country music.

As with *White Ladder*, the album would be released in Ireland (on IHT on 23 June 2000) several months before Britain, whose audience was deemed to still be catching up with *White Ladder*. Gray realised however that it was "bound to get stuck in the front of the record shops, because retailers have seen our last record do so much. But I want people to perceive very clearly that we haven't got down to following our creative twistings from the last thing yet. As far as the stripped-down approach to the recording goes, it just seemed appropriate; for the people who liked the earlier stuff, I suppose it's a bit of a treat."

Much of the material on *Songs* reflected the unhappy phase of Gray's life, previously hinted at on *Sell, Sell, Sell*, when his career appeared to be going nowhere and his parents split up. "It was a while ago now but, yeah, everything went a bit weird," he admits. "It shattered the family unit and the situation became completely fragmented, which is disorientating. I questioned a lot of things about what the past had been like: had I just been missing the point?"

He concluded that he'd been "living in cloud cuckoo land. Your parents, whether you consciously put them on a pedestal or not, are still your parents. When you suddenly see them as people, and they're acting in such a way that you're feeling more grown-up than they are, it's like what the fuck's going on here? Then they split up, sell the house, one's over here with a new bloke and suddenly there's no home either. I remember going back to a couple of particularly miserable occasions and thinking, 'Fuck, I'm out on my own here.' It comes home to you what your existence is all about. But I won't pontificate more or drag out family details. It did happen and it did have a profound impact on me, although I think I've recovered from it. It just changed my perspective."

He would, in future, resist "fantasise (that) things are better or more idyllic than they are. It's easy to live in cloud cuckoo land or just not to see." The running order of *Lost Songs* was originally so "downbeat, with real wrist-slitting songs" that his wife, Olivia, used to say "turn it off, it's depressing me!" Gray re-sequenced the tracks "balancing acoustic recordings against, say, instrumentals that have flecks of sunlight to lift the listener!"

Either way, the overall mood of the album reflected a "depressing" period in Gray's life. "As my career nose-dived, my family life dipped as well. Not in terms of my wife but the Grays. I was on the road a lot, nothing was working out and I was becoming less sure of the things I thought I'd been 100 per cent sure about. My own heart. The world I was living in. What I was doing. My family. How everything fitted together. The fact that my original family was falling apart certainly made me ask questions about what was real about the relationship my parents had. And what wasn't. During my childhood, did I buy into a sweetened version of family life? I always thought it was great but maybe I missed something vital in their relationship."

The album opened promisingly enough with 'Flame Turns Blue'. a highlight of the live show (and an encore at many) that had finally made it onto tape. One of the few songs to receive a full band arrangement, its particularly Dylan-esque introduction led to a song that, with its freight trains and lemon trees, seemed clearly set in America.

The lyrical inspiration, he revealed, came from his relationship with his mother. "My mum and dad had been split up for a couple of years and my mum was about to start seeing another bloke and I remember thinking she seemed really vulnerable and what a big deal this was," he said. "All she'd been through and then to stake it all on someone else again. The courage you need to do that. Those thoughts also occurred while I was writing the song that opens this album."

Rumours circulated that 'Flame Turns Blue' would be sent as a single to the Irish market. This would have been logical since a promo sent to radio stations to promote the album received serious airplay, but it was not to happen.

The simple, sparse 'Twilight' was a track he identified as "maybe slightly down, but still lit with the kind of excitement and wonder I find as I breathe in the world I move through." The song was so sparingly accompanied by acoustic guitar it was probably the nearest to an acappella Gray fans would have heard. The title phrase cropped up in the first line only, leaving 'Little darlin'/Till I see you once again' as the hook, with a 'na na na' playout evoking Van Morrison yet again.

Track three, 'Hold On', continued the solitary mood, and is almost painfully brief, the briefest of a brief (37-minute) album at just a shade under two minutes. David is offering solace to a girl who's left her lover and is unreasonably, in his view, blaming herself. But the boot is soon on the other foot with 'As I'm Leaving', a song that captured one Internet reviewer's heart. "Anyone who adores a songwriter's ability to capture that space between sadness and hopefulness and nurture it into a blanket of comfort will curl up with this song over and over again."

For David Gray, the key line summing up his inspiration was 'throw my heart out on the stones' – something he'd done all too often in the struggling pre-*White Ladder* years. "I had years of being hammered by everything, and that's exactly what it's like. It's too painful to be putting yourself out all the time to the indifference or the casual slagging or being totally ignored. One doesn't feel good about it. It's hard to 'remain philosophical'. So you carry a bit of a defence mechanism – cynicism and so on.

"That's becoming an inappropriate way to deal with things now. I'm having to open myself up to a world where people have run away with the whole thing, and it's not mine anymore. Even though I didn't put any particular ceiling on it, I suppose I didn't think it would go this far. And I do think everyone's pleased for me. Success through failure – there's a great story there."

The stark, guitar and vocal 'If Your Love Is Real' was a track questioning the permanence of relationships. "It's about someone falling for somebody and some mad, passionate thing that is fantastic, in-and-out of bed, then they're off somewhere else and you're wondering whether it was just a good time for them or if they really feel as deeply as you do." As the song progressed, a subtle wash of electric piano softened the mood only slightly as he concluded that no matter what, his love was real and that was all that mattered.

The plucked guitar figure of 'Tidal Wave' sped through what seems to be a throwaway track by Gray's own standards. The line "Coming over Waterloo" nodded to Ray Davies' 'Waterloo Sunset', but there was little else there to make an impact in a song he performed solo and was over in a mere two minutes and 20 seconds.

'Falling Down The Mountainside' is considered by many to be the key track of *Songs*. Gray revealed he'd recorded a version at New York's Electric Ladyland studios, when he was still with EMI, just before embarking on the disastrous summer tour of '96. "It was inspired by somebody I know committing suicide. . . When I wrote the first two lines, the rest of the song came quickly. . . The song is more eloquent than I would be." Presumably this explains the bracketed 'For Stephen' in the title. Whatever, the song gathered a gentle momentum with a tumbling piano figure and drums entering halfway through proceedings. "You left me cold to meet your ghost all over town," Gray complained, admitting the first thing he'd do if his friend came back would be knock him down.

The guitar-led instrumental 'January Rain' acted as a palate freshener before the vitriolic lyric of 'Red Moon' gave notice that this was an album with teeth after all. With its "weighing silver/every kiss must have a price" metaphors, this was clearly another page from his scrapbook of unhappy romances.

The closing 'Clean Pair Of Eyes' was written at a time when he wondered if he'd ever get another recording deal after the demise of the EMI link. He was in New York with Clune, and it was a visit to the Metropolitan Art Museum that bucked up his spirits. "It was the kind of day where you feel you're seeing the world for the first time.

It was super-real. Then I saw a painting by Vermeer. He was painting with light. It was the most iridescent form of perfection. I couldn't believe it!" That night he started writing 'Clean Pair Of Eyes', finishing it in Ireland as a celebration of "that sense of transformation (which) is what I hope to fire with my music."

Since the timing of *Lost Songs* closely approximated the 20 minutes per side of the now-outmoded vinyl format, several songs fans had keenly awaited were, inevitably, omitted from the final result – victims of Gray's fanatical quality control. One notable omission was 'Tell Me More Lies', which had been featured on the *Hot Press* 1999 annual compilation CD and was therefore presumably discounted.

"A few of the songs had failed to make it onto *White Ladder* because they didn't quite fit," Gray explained, "while others were written just after *Sell, Sell, Sell*. So they had fallen through the cracks so we swept them up with the broom of music and now they've been collected on this album."

Music Today's Heather Croteau was typical of the album's favourable reviewers. "While this album is musically slimmer than *White Ladder*, it is rich with a soulful honesty that fans have come to savour. *Lost Songs* will teach listeners about the formative years in the life of their new friend David Gray. The record will also help to explain who he is and how he has come so far."

Lost Songs arrival at the top of the Irish chart inspired David to send out an Internet message to his fans. Its breathless tone sums up the rollercoaster ride he clearly felt he was on. "The year 2000 began with a most bizarre, fantastic and totally unforeseen event. The album *White Ladder* went to Number 1 in the Irish charts and, as if this was not enough, then proceeded to install itself for a six-week stay. There and then, it became obvious to me that I was going to have to stop putting a ceiling on my expectations. The rules were being re-written, and what has happened in the six months that has followed, has only served to strengthen my belief that I have entered a realm where anything is possible.

"So to the release of *Lost Songs*. Songs from the lean years, years when I was dragging my music like a burden through an indifferent world, feeding my creative spirit on scraps.

"My how the world has changed, and so quickly! These days, when

I take to the stage I am singing in another world entirely, and I am filled to bursting with an irrepressible joy at being alive and doing what I'm supposed to do.

"So as *Lost Songs* leaps in straight at Number 1, it seems like the right time to stop the wheels for a moment, and say thank you to all the people who have taken my music to their hearts, bought the records, and cheered at the concerts. The circle is complete, what was lost is now found."

CHAPTER 10

The Future

If 2000 had been "like three years rolled into one. Life in fast-forward," for David Gray, the first year of the new millennium would, to quote Neil Young, turn out to be more a Journey Through The Past. After *Lost Songs 95–98* brought his recent past to life in the British marketplace, Virgin/Hut finally reissued his first two efforts as well as a compilation album made up of the first three singles (or EPs – Extended Play records – as they somewhat archaically termed them). Then a US tour had been set up to establish him there as a headlining artist, playing to an audience that would doubtless expect the majority of *White Ladder* to be served up as fresh as when it had been recorded fully three years earlier.

Gray admitted he found this time displacement a strain. "The last year or so has been so different from the rest of my career," he sighed. "When I put a record out before, I worked it for at least a month before it went off the radio and no one was interested in it. Then it was back to the drawing board to make another one. But I've been working this album for years. There's been so much promo and so many interviews. There's always things to do, from the moment I get up."

Age was, this chain-smoking thirty-something explained, fast catching up on him. "I found my physical limit this year. I've always worked hard. . . but never at this pace. I was exhausted, then I got scared. It's the idea that the youthful, invulnerable quality is no longer; I've shed a skin.

"The amount of talking I've had to do about *White Ladder*. . . Christ! It seems a little bizarre to be recalling things from the past. But because the thing is still expanding, you have to do it, I can't say no. I've had many, many, many hundreds of serious interviews about this record – too many, to be honest."

But the biggest cause for introspection and retrospection came in February 2001 with the death of his father from cancer. This understandably caused a rearrangement of his tour plans, though such was the momentum of his career right now that he had little time to brood on things.

Though Peter Gray had been ill for nine months, and David had cancelled four dates on his summer 2000 US tour to be with him during surgery, he would show up at gigs even when he was undergoing chemotherapy. "He was probably my biggest fan," David confirmed, "which made me uncomfortable at times because he was so excited about the whole thing that he wanted to tell everyone. . ."

Rolling Stone magazine had sent a writer over to London to get the inside story on the lifestyle of the 'new star' as Gray prepared to take on the States. They followed him around, even tagging along to a Sunday lunchtime assignation with Radio 1's Jamie Theakston. Gray was understandably still coming to terms with his recent bereavement, but, while holding back the tears, paid smiling tribute to his late parent. "My dad was up for anything. He came to Glastonbury. He was bloody bonkers. He was having chemotherapy at the time, and he came down into the dressing room chanting, 'Chemo! Chemo! Chemo!' He was pissed out of his head, basically.

"My dad has died, there's a lot to be learned, it's an enriching experience," he continued. "Fucking hell, that's what life is about, as trite as it may sound. It's impossible to avoid all the clichés. But, you know, life's a bit of a mess, isn't it?" Understandably the European tour due to kick off at Madrid Caracol on 28 February, and wind up in Paris on 8 March was postponed due to the bereavement, but a spokesperson emphasised that his US tour was not in jeopardy. Tellingly, when the British Society of Songwriters,

Composers and Authors awarded him his Ivor, David accepted it while expressing the opinion that his late father "would have been over the moon" about it.

Given his youthful soccer prowess, and fanaticism for Manchester United, David had been a natural choice to be invited to the *New Musical Express* Carling Cup, a five-a-side football tournament held at the Crystal Palace National Indoor Arena. "Irish minstrel David" as the publicity labelled him would have been sharing the spotlight with West Country rockers Reef, fellow Mancunian (and former Take That heartthrob) Mark Owen and indie-punk faves Idlewild. Ex-pro stars dusting off their boots to participate in aid of a children's charity included a pair of ex-Red Devils in Neil Webb and Mickey Thomas.

Amazing as it seemed, though, David's celebrity now eclipsed these former international footballers. And he was acclimatising slowly to the delights and perils of being recognised in the street. "There's definitely going to be some sort of collision between this and my life as I've had it for the past ten years. I've got used to wandering around doing my own thing. Now it looks like this insane sort of success will start and it will, I'm sure, bring its own stresses. I've very little interest in being a celebrity. Zero, in fact."

That New Year's Eve, he'd recounted, he had been out and about in fancy dress – "a musketeer-style thing and a false moustache, all this crap, a wig – in a pub in the middle of nowhere, and this guy says, 'David Gray! I love your stuff!' Over Christmas, I walked onto the platform at Kentish Town tube station, and directly opposite was a poster of me. I was wearing the same coat, and there was this bloke sitting down, looking at the poster and looking at me. I just burst out laughing."

Finally, the success of *White Ladder* had blotted out the bad memories of the cock-ups, lack of promotion and false studio starts. "All that Paul Kimble (*Sell, Sell, Sell*) stuff and the heartache that led me there – I'm gonna have to let it go now. I've been a battler; an infantryman, and now it feels like I've been promoted to sergeant."

But with success had come a staunching of his creative flow. "On show days, there's soundcheck, and there's no room for creative thinking. I've found that my creative process has about stopped. But when I stop touring for a week or so, it starts again straight away."

And that was fortunate indeed, as it was reported he was in negotiation to write the soundtrack for a new film, *Serendipity*. Directed by and starring American actor John Cusack, it seemed this would hit the screen sometime before Christmas. With David's current and ever-unrelenting schedule, however, it might not be worth putting money on which Christmas this would be...

The film would feature Cusack playing a man who meets up with an old college flame, Kate Beckinsale (of *Pearl Harbour* fame), with each on the verge of marriage to someone else. For temporary purposes (and with the singer's permission), they had taken a couple of the tracks from the *Lost Songs* album and used them to accompany the rough cut. "They work so well in this particular film that they want me to do more. I'm hoping it comes off. I'd really like to write some new songs for the film, and that could happen. But you know what movies are like; it's a haphazard, political game. Once the record companies come in and someone buys the rights to the soundtrack, you don't know what's going to happen. But I think it could be a great thing to do."

But a soundtrack album would be of less interest to his ever-growing army of fans than the fully-fledged successor to *White Ladder*. It would be some sort of victory if, next time he released a front-line album, it could receive simultaneous exposure. He had indeed become a prisoner of his success. "As an artist, I want to go and make my next record, I don't want to go and sing this one for another year. But there's something stronger at work. My career's taken off. This shit doesn't happen twice. We're on a roll and you can't stop it."

Gray and his band had committed some demos to tape before setting off on the American tour and were so excited about them they devised arrangements "to give the songs a bit of an airing on the road." He'd got half a dozen finished songs and twice as many ideas. "*White Ladder* liberated me from worrying about being taken seriously. Now we have that – and I think the next one will be the record. I think it might end being quite... mad."

Meanwhile, in the awaiting States, Gray-mania was running high. *White Ladder*, which had become a fixture in the *Billboard* Top 50, went platinum in February and anticipation of the 2001 tour was high. Most impressively, tickets for the 6,500-capacity New York Radio City Music Hall sold out in just one hour when they went on sale – the prerogative of an established star rather than an up and coming artist.

And the up and coming artist was taken aback by his burgeoning popularity. "I've been amazed with the way tickets have sold," he confessed. "Shows have been selling out all over – Boston and two nights in San Francisco took like 20 minutes. We're just blown away. When you hear that kind of thing, that brings it home more than anything. We're entering into a real cauldron of expectation, and there's going to be a real buzz in the air. Nothing makes you feel better than that."

Meanwhile, *Lost Songs 95–98* made its debut on the British mainland, having been available to Irish consumers for over six months. It entered the chart at Number 7, its triple-platinum predecessor having slipped three to Number 16. After an early-March week in which they nestled cheek by jowl at Numbers 12 and 13, the pair then traded places, *Ladder* rising to seven and *Lost Songs* slipping to 14. The newcomer had, however, acquired another gold disc for David's wall by this point.

It would maintain its Top 20 status for six weeks, finally slipping out of the all-important 75 in its 11th week on sale. But with only a brief advertising campaign behind it and no single released, *Lost Songs* had enjoyed its brief moment of glory. It was destined to remain a low-profile release for people to discover rather than have thrust under their noses. Gray's first producer, Dave Armstrong, certainly wasn't surprised by his former charge's reversion to singer-songwriter type. "Yeah, I think it's probably where his heart lies, with the very early stuff, though I haven't spoken to him recently at all."

In a throwback to events earlier in his career, and possibly emboldened by *Lost Songs'* chart success, he even threw caution to the wind and played a handful of solo acoustic dates without his band. "It's weird, because it was how I started out, and it was really strange going back to it," said Gray. "Great in a certain way, because you have a total freedom, but I realised how much I'd changed. I've adapted to having a band, and it was weird not having them around. It takes a little while to get back into that whole standing-on-your-own thing."

137

Indeed, one of these solo dates had opened the year at Joe's Pub in New York City where a denim-clad Gray had started his 14-song set at the grand piano. 'Please Forgive Me' found him, in the words of one critic, "closing his eyes, shaking his head and banging out the sparse chords like Ray Charles on speed." This gig was recorded by Jeff Juliano, a sound engineer/producer who had worked on most of the Dave Matthews Band's live releases. Juliano's personal website included *David Gray: Live At Joe's Pub* as a title he'd been involved with, suggesting a US release of some kind might have been planned.

The instrumental flourishes that had punctuated *White Ladder* were absent in a gig David laughingly compared to "the pub shows I used to play years ago – but with people." 'White Ladder', 'My Oh My' and 'Sail Away' had seemed unusually bare, but the presence of 'All The Love' made up for it. This new song had been débuted on the 2000 UK tour, and, in a band situation, it wasn't unusual for David to throw in lines from Led Zeppelin's 'Black Dog'. The uniqueness of the solo setting wasn't lost on Gray. "I'm taking tonight as an opportunity to play things I don't get to play very often or that in fact I haven't played at all."

The set closer 'Babylon' ensured he would return – but few could have predicted his choice of encore song, a hastily busked 'Streets Of Philadelphia'. "Christ, I should've worked out the chords. . . bollocks!" he excused himself before strumming Bruce Springsteen's poignant film theme song with its questioning chorus: "Will you receive me brother with your faithless kiss/Or will we leave each other alone like this?"

'Sail Away', from *White Ladder*, was receiving national US exposure on the soundtrack to Robert De Niro's new movie, *15 Minutes*, while second single 'Please Forgive Me' was about to be supplied to radio and video outlets, even though the video for its predecessor, 'Babylon', was still getting exposure on both the 'adult' cable channel VH1 and its hipper sisters, MTV and M2.

In recent weeks Gray had hardly been off the screen, performing on *Saturday Night Live, The Late Show With David Letterman* (twice), *The Tonight Show With Jay Leno, Late Late Show With Craig Kilborn* and *Austin City Limits.* And, as if all that weren't enough, press support was being received from magazines as diverse as *Rolling Stone, USA Today, Newsweek, Spin* and *Entertainment Weekly.*

So all was set fair when the North American tour, largest of his four since the March 2000 release of *White Ladder*, kicked off at Minneapolis Quest Club on 12 April. The 36-date itinerary included Los Angeles' Universal Amphitheatre, as well as multiple engagements at The Warfield in San Francisco and the Moore Theatre in Seattle which rounded off the tour – except for a sole excursion across the Canadian border – in late June.

It had been reported that David would be the special guest of U2 in certain states, but in the event this was not to be. Opening the show for him, instead, was the diminutive Canadian hip-hopette Nelly Furtado, a precocious 22 year-old of Portuguese extraction whose hit 'I'm Like A Bird' had won the approval of Elton John, among others. Though both were arguably singer-songwriters with attitude, the *San Francisco Chronicle,* reviewing the first of two sold-out gigs at the city's Warfield Theatre, underlined the fact that it was in many ways a mis-match.

"Perky to the point of pesty, Furtado is exactly what Gray isn't, a melange of different styles and musical ideas – say, Brazilian rhythms set against hip-hop beats and a DJ scratching – without any real character of her own. Gray, on the other hand, appears to be a unique phenomenon – a genuine article, an authentic musician. Let's hope for a trend." Furtado's single success with 'I'm Like A Bird' would see her depart the tour for dates in her own right.

Their paths would cross again in Scotland in July's T In the Park festival, when ironically the pair would perform simultaneously on different stages. In other dates, up and coming songstress Shea Seger filled in, while an alternative opening act was provided by Fisher, a duo made up of singer-songwriter Kathy Fisher and multi-instrumentalist Ron Wasserman.

The shows were sometimes received rapturously, other times in reverent near-silence when the set contained less *White Ladder* material than usual. Varying the set in this way certainly appealed to the amateur concert taping fraternity, whose computer-burned CDs were traded avidly with fellow fans. Not only did they get new songs, but a relatively noise-free recording.

Up to eight new songs made an appearance in the set list – and while David recognised the risk of adding too much unfamiliar material when many first-time fans had come to see him on the basis of *White Ladder* alone, he let previous experience guide him in his decision. "Whether they'll all be played each night is another story, but we'll be bringing them to freshen up the set. It's the dawning of a new era, and stepping into the next phase a bit. It's like pre–production for the next album in a way. I'm obviously fond of all of them, but I will literally wait and see how the audience takes to them."

He recalled performing 'Babylon' several years earlier, when he'd just written it. "I did it in a very simple way, but it had such a massive effect on the audience from the very first time we ever played it. A song they'd never heard before. We played it in Ireland on a couple of shows, and it went down like a storm. We thought, 'We've got something here.' You never really know (how good they are) until you get an objective opinion, and there's no better objective opinion than from 2,000 screaming maniacs."

The opening night of the tour in Minneapolis had seen three new songs: 'Real Love', 'Be Mine' (its first public airing) and 'The Longest Time', in the set, with 'Last Boat To America' (with David on piano) as the first of four encores and 'All The Love', seguing into Zeppelin's 'Black Dog', as the last.

Jon Bream, reporter for the local *Star/Tribune*, rated the newcomers thus: "'Real Love' was bright and poppy, like U2 sans electric guitar. 'Be Mine' suggested Rod Stewart stuck in first gear, singing words by Donovan. 'The Longest Time' evoked a Van Morrison lyric delivered by Elton John. 'Northern Sea' (presumably 'Last Boat To America'), the best of the unrecorded stuff, was moody, atmospheric and almost mystical before ending with a loud, intense Irish jam."

Even such time-honoured favourites as 'This Year's Love' were rested on occasion – though at the LA gig David reinstated it to the set-list at short notice when Clune went to take off his shirt. Finding it impossible to play the next scheduled number, 'Please Forgive Me' without his drummer, he played the ballad to swoons from the female section of the audience.

Fans who'd aligned themselves with David on his previous, more intimate excursions reported him often too tired to come out and socialise after gigs as had once been his habit. A fierce internet post-ing war raged, but wise counsels eventually prevailed: "By the way," one still-supportive fan insisted, "in the earlier days (and until very recently) DG and the boys were super-friendly after gigs and would chat at the bar for ages after the smaller gigs. He replied to a letter I wrote once as well, so don't get all 'Stan'* on him just because times have changed and success has come."

For his part, David admitted that the ravages of touring had hit him harder than ever this time. "You get so tired, I get so permanently tired. The only time I feel normal is after the show. You're on an adrenaline cycle, and come out of being tired and feel normal after-wards because of the rush. I have tried to look after myself on this tour and watched what I ate, tried not to smoke too much. But I have been exhausted. I don't know the answer, I'm wondering why myself."

A gig at the Boathouse in Norfolk, Virginia (Dave Matthews Band territory) brought an incident of note. In the middle of 'We're Not Right', David broke out in a huge grin. Afterwards, he said, "I think I just had a *moment*. I was looking out in the audience and saw a six-year-old girl singing along to the words of my song. They start them young down here."

The first of the two New York shows had been remarkable for its restraint. Only half a dozen of the audience had been moved to take to their feet, so on the second night David issued his permission to participate on a more physical level. "I command you to stand, New York," he ordered – and the opening chords of 'Babylon' that fol-lowed had the desired effect. He also dedicated the new 'Last Boat To America' to his father, a rare public expression of his feelings. 'Gathering Dust' from his first album was also pulled out of the bag for a final encore, even though it had not been on the set list.

The 23 May gig at San Francisco's Warfield Theatre was taped and filmed for possible future release. The Warfield was a regular venue for bands about to break big, last year's British invaders having included The Stereophonics and The Charlatans (or Charlatans UK as they are known). And though the venue was in a downmarket part of town

★ 'Stan', of course, was the Eminem song about an obsessive fan.

where ticket touts and street vendors rubbed shoulders with hookers and drug dealers, Gray attracted an enthusiastic full house.

Former cohort David Nolté had meanwhile returned to the West Coast, where he was working with LA bands like the Wondermints, the Jigsaw Seen and Candypants, as well as teaming with Kinks guitarist Dave Davies. "I've done everything from being his guitar tech to playing guitar, bass, keys and harmonica to recording him in my home studio."

Nolté admitted he was "very surprised at the extent of his former boss's success. I was not surprised by the success in Ireland because I had toured with him over there and knew how he touched those people, but to break through all over, especially in the US given the current state of popular music is totally amazing. It's so left field that it almost makes sense."

With the Eighties the latest era to attract the burgeoning rock-'n'roll nostalgia market, Soft Cell had re-formed to play some warmly received gigs. Had the success of David's version of 'Say Hello, Wave Goodbye' played any part in Marc Almond and David Ball's decision to reunite? They didn't say, but Almond confessed he'd had to stop running from his hit parade history. "At some point, you have to face your past and embrace it. People are always going to play that record, they're going to identify that record ('Say Hello. . .') with me, so I look at it as being a theme song. I can look back and say, 'I've made a record that's really been a part of people's lives.' It was part of their soundtrack. It was a piece of musical history. A piece of pop culture. Like it or not, it was a unique and original record, and people still like it, even today."

In an interview with Ian Shirley for the magazine *Record Buyer*, Almond was asked more directly about Gray's cover version, and the response was warmly affirmative. "It was fantastic! How can I complain about that? That one song has probably saved my life this past year (laughs). It's paid off the taxman, kept the taxman happy, it's got me on an even keel. I spent three years trying to pay off debts in my life from my 10–15 years of drug abuse and wanton behaviour. Unreliability and this that and the other.

"I worked so hard the last few years to get myself on an even keel, and along comes David Gray and saves me. I think it's fantastic and a great thrill when someone covers one of your songs." Almond also admitted that it was "the song I love most of all of mine," his biggest hit 'Tainted Love' having been written by someone else. When David Gray was asked in an Internet web-chat in mid 2001 who he'd like to do a duet with in the future, he revealed: "I've been asked to do one this summer, and I suggested Marc Almond."

Talking of music with electronic bleeps and squiggles, David's services had been acquired by stablemates Orbital. It was time to repay the remix favour and make a cameo appearance on 'Illuminate', a track from their new album *The Altogether*. Paul Hartnoll revealed to *Q* magazine (who'd been blissfully unaware of the family connection via Phil's wife) he had "whole tracks of him singing on my hard disk, things he wasn't sure what to do with. There's pretty much an album's worth of stuff." You wouldn't want to erase that, suggested the streetwise scribe. "No, you wouldn't," agreed Paul – "with a ruefulness to suggest that's exactly what he has done," the magazine concluded.

In fact, the younger Hartnoll appears to have been winding the style bible up in a big way. Brother Phil was far more specific when talking to *Making Music* magazine. "We normally work without mates and rarely collaborate with people we've never met," he began, explaining that they'd known David for years. "Basically we share managers and my wife and his are sisters so he's sort of my brother in law and uncle to my children. He's been in the family for ages, he's got a great voice."

Getting down to the musical nitty gritty, Phil, revealed that 'Illuminate' had been kicking around for the best part of a year and a half, and was one of two collaborations they'd attempted. "He sung on that track ages ago, but we never got it right. But now we have. Also he came round and sang a song into our computer. That one's still there – a truly 'Lost Song'." Everything had been entered into on a casual basis. "We wrote that track and always felt it needed a male vocal," Phil said. "And he just popped round one day – he used to live around the corner from us and it was like, really casual, 'Hey Dave! Have a go at this. See if you come up with anything.' And he came up with that and it's like 'Wow, that's good. That works'."

David was slightly embarrassed at all the fuss over a cut he considered a throwaway track. "They're friends of mine, so I just went in and did some singing in their studio for an afternoon and it ended up going on their record. I wish I could have worked on it a bit more, to be honest. I didn't know it was going to become such an important thing. But, it was interesting."

David's companion in the guest-star stakes was Tom Baker, one of several actors to have played Dr Who (Orbital's 'jungle-style' version of the TV show's theme having long been a stage favourite.) 'The Altogether' entered the chart in mid-May at a respectable Number 11, five places above *White Ladder* which was also celebrating chart week one. . . of a second year.

Soundtrack possibilities or not, the odds still were that, when David Gray finally re-entered a recording studio, it would be to record a new album proper. "I've got some studio time pencilled in sometime in 2004," he joked, confessing that it might prove difficult to recapture the previous spirit of spontaneity knowing there will be millions of people the world over waiting to listen to it. One thing was for sure, though – success wouldn't change his way of working.

"I'd want to continue along the same lines, and I can't imagine that it's going to be a problem to make another heartfelt record. We're not twiddling our thumbs thinking about how we can emulate the success of 'Babylon'. We feel the new ideas will take care of themselves," he said. "But I think I've got better records (than *White Ladder*)."

Manager Rob Holden agreed. "I don't believe David's made his best record yet, but we'll have to make sure he's got enough space to develop comfortably. If we wanted to do well in the Pacific Rim we could keep touring *White Ladder* for the next two years, but that would be a mistake. There's an energy there that can only be sustained if we keep moving on."

But moving on wouldn't prove as easy as all that. Hut Records chose July 2001 to recoup some of the losses they'd incurred when they had a pre-fame David Gray on their books. Not only were they re-releasing *A Century Ends* and *Flesh* but were issuing a totally new release entitled *The EPs 92–94*. Far from being outraged by these events, however, David had given his full permission and had also contributed the following sleevenotes.

"If you like I was working in black and white when I was just with the acoustic guitar back then, and that was what I was best at. There were times later on, working with a full palate when it all went awry. Some of the things on here I think are the best representations of that early time 'cos I'm just standing there on my own. 'Birds Without Wings', 'L's Song' and 'Lovers' in particular I think are very successful – they still stand up."

The first half-dozen tracks wrapped up the two initial three-trackers, 'Birds Without Wings'/'L's Song'/'The Light' and 'Shine'/'Brick Walls'/'The Rice'. The A-sides were included for completeness' sake even though they were available on album. The summer 1993 release 'Wisdom'/'Lovers'/'4am' came next, while 'Coming Down' from *Flesh* rounded out the audio content of the disc, even though this had only been included on promo singles.

The packaging could have been termed classic in its economy. It aped the elements of the first two albums, combining the mono-chrome simplicity of the first with the final laughing picture of the *Flesh* booklet that formed the new front cover. Stills were included from the 'Shine' video which, along with that for 'Wisdom', was included as a multi-media bonus. Chart-wise, it enjoyed a single week at Number 68, but it was largely unadvertised and achieved this on word of mouth alone.

Producer Dave Anderson, also unaware of its appearance, vowed to "go and buy a copy. I did see that in the shops but I didn't realise what was on it. I noticed people were clamouring to get hold of the early records. Letters were written to places and things. . . where can I get hold of these things?" Anderson also had an interest in Virgin/Hut's reissue of *A Century Ends*. "Obviously since he became so hugely popular I was wondering why they hadn't re-released it. It seemed like a golden opportunity, and now they have. I remember thinking at the time it was a great record. . . which it probably still is, I haven't listened to it much but I remember being hugely disappointed when it was lost in the great sea of the music business."

The releases gave David the chance to reflect on how much he had changed as a person and as a musician over the intervening years. "An awful lot! Obviously age has a mellowing process, slightly more gradual on some people than others. I have a different approach (now). I used to be like a bull in a china shop. I had all the best intentions, but sometimes you have to take a step back and relax. You cannot force the issue the whole time. With *White Ladder* I enjoyed the experience more. I relaxed and let it happen and it came out so much better."

He was surprised to find how downbeat the releases had been, in parts at least. "God, I thought I was a happy, chipper chap and then I listen to the early stuff. The anger! There seemed to be a lot to be angry about, I don't think it was a bad thing, but it shocks me when I hear it. There was obviously real anger at the fact that no-one was listening, or maybe it was insecurity. But believe me, I wasn't really like that. Not at all."

The new, improved, mellow David Gray was planning to invest some of his new-found wealth in a new house. Not that he planned to move that far: the Camden Town and Primrose Hill suburbs of North London were not a million miles away from his current Stoke Newington neighbourhood. By now he had abandoned his legendary home studio, transferring the equipment into a unit in a quiet industrial complex elsewhere in London.

As for the future, "I'd like to start a family and settle down, and at some point, that will become more viable and attractive than another tour of America. It's a great life, but there will be a point where I will want to do something else, maybe paint again or, I don't know, spend £200,000 on my bathroom, those things you do when you are a rock star! But I don't think I will ever want to stop making music, writing songs or performing live. If everyone is up for a good time, we'll give them a good time."

He was well aware that fame would mean more than his share of unwanted attention, and was prepared however reluctantly to live behind locked gates to retain his privacy. As for how incipient parenthood was, no-one was saying: he intimated to *Rolling Stone* that he was happy enjoying life with Olivia and their friends, throwing mad dinner parties where the soundtrack would range from Diana Ross through Kraftwerk to Nirvana. "It always ends with Nirvana."

Lyrically it seemed his own songs would continue to grow simpler, relying on raw emotion rather than the wordy narrative of his early work. "I learned that the more you have to say, perhaps the simpler you need to be saying it. As life teaches you lessons, it strips away the fussy detail, and just suggesting things or leaving a space to let someone read between the lines is a very powerful tool."

He cited Frank Sinatra – specifically the track, 'Quiet Nights Of Quiet Stars' from his 1967 collaboration with Brazilian composer Antonio Carlos Jobim – as exemplifying what he was striving for: "Mind-blowing lyrics, ultimately simple. I want to say things in the most simple way." Asked whether he has a songwriting rule, he responded, "Less adjectives."

He felt he was missing out on music he should be listening to, R&B (in the modern sense of the term) getting his vote when he did find the time. "I've got friends that make me tapes with more dance or groove-y kind of things, 'cause I'm never gonna have the time to go and find what you're supposed to listen to. I've bought TLC and that kind of skippy, kind of swing-beat stuff just to listen to the production." Other purchases included Lambchop's *Nixon*, plus recent release from The Eels and Flaming Lips.

Two days prior to his European tour, David played Glastonbury again. In fact, the year 2001 would provide farmer Michael Eavis with a well-earned break, but in its place a Virtual Glastonbury was broadcast over the Internet at the site www.playlouder.com with David as the cyber event's opening act. Live sets from Basement Jaxx, Stereophonics and Gorillaz topped off each day.

David Gray had become a byword for thoughtful songs, passionately delivered – and three very different examples, interestingly all female, reared their heads in 2001 to prove it. Irish singer Juliet Turner, whose independently release *Burn The Black Suit* was attempting to do a *White Ladder,* used David to reject the suggestion that female artists tend to open their hearts and bare their souls more readily than their male counterparts. "I just don't think it's true at all," she insisted. "Look at David Gray, he's always baring his soul, isn't he?"

The next was from a less likely source. Pop band Steps were publicly mulling over their plans for when they eventually split. While boys Lee Latchford Evans and Ian 'H' Watkins wanted to tread the boards as actors and Claire Richards set her sights on a TV presenter's job, Faye Tozer (the tall, blonde one) was keen to develop her songwriting skills. "I'm really enjoying writing. I find it difficult to write pop though – my stuff is more storytelling like David Gray," she said.

Last but not least came a new Christian Tattersfield protégé, Kathryn Roberts, who was set to undergo the transformation 'from critically acclaimed singer-songwriter to platinum-selling mainstream success,' according to music trade journal *Music Week* in August 2001. Headlining the piece 'Williams eyes David Gray rulebook for major deal', the publication quoted the singer as saying: "I think the main similarity between me and David is that there is someone like Christian in a big music machine that has this sort of vision."

Williams had, like Gray, already sold a fair few albums (40,000) independently, and her single 'Jasmine Hoop' was to be revamped a la 'Babylon' with radio play in mind. "If you listen to the version of 'Babylon' on *White Ladder* it's not an immediate hit," said Tattersfield, who concluded that "for people who like Travis and Coldplay, there aren't actually many albums they can buy. We knew *White Ladder* would explode if we could expose it alongside such albums." Whether he could repeat the trick and Williams emulate her role model's success remained to be seen.

For the original David Gray, festivals remained the best way to be seen by as many people as possible. The end of June therefore brought engagements at the St Gallen and Werchter Festivals in Switzerland and Belgium, crossing the border for a brace of German dates in Stuttgart and Hamburg.

The summer of 2001 found David back on the festival circuit. July brought a return to Scotland's annual outdoor 'biggie' T In The Park where he was second top of the main stage bill for the first night (headliners being Stereophonics). Next came London's Hyde Park before a return to the continent eight days later for the Montreux Jazz Festival. The eighteenth and nineteenth would see him playing the two V2001 Festivals at Weston Park, Leeds, and Chelmsford.

Nor had he forgotten his adopted home city, scheduling an outdoor date at Dublin's Smithfield Market on 19 July which would rapidly escalate to three dates and a change of venue. Three gigs were to be played back to back on July 19, 20 and 21 in Dublin's Inner City with local heroes The Frames in support. David had namechecked the Frames' Glen Hansard – then a recent veteran of *The Commitments* film band – as far back as 1994 as one of his favourite songwriters, so it's likely they were a personal choice. The first two dates had been sold out for many weeks, and the decision was made at a late stage to move to Marlay Park. Fans criticised this as profiteering (the Smithfield is variously estimated as holding between 8–10,000 people) but it seemed many of the other concerts scheduled had been moved in response to local residents' complaints. The T in The Park had proved a winning performance, the running order reading like a slightly revised version of the album – to the audience's evident delight. After softening them up, Gray announced that "this is where the fun begins" and played a revved up version of 'Please Forgive Me'. "The drummer has been keyed up all along but this is his excuse to get really carried away, whilst David Gray keeps up his head shaking throughout the entire performance," noted one happy reviewer who awarded the performance a full five stars.

Whether it was the effect of playing to these large audiences unfamiliar with his music or possibly the airplay gained by the otherwise disappointing (chart-wise) 'Sail Away' can't be certain, but the second week of August 2001 saw *White Ladder* take that last, hitherto elusive step up to the chart summit. This was just a week after the British Phonographic Industry had certified it five times platinum (1.5 million UK sales).

"We've been sort of vindicated, really," he commented. "It's done really well and given us a new-found confidence to just sort of relax even further and really enjoy the whole thing. . . rather than feel any pressure. Just get in there and really enjoy making the next record, really have a good laugh."

East West's selection of 'This Years Love' as David's next UK single release, was deliberate and signalled to the British public that there were more facets to David Gray than the dancey Orbital re-mixes of 'Babylon' and 'Please Forgive Me' had shown. The song's chart performance inevitably failed to live up to 'Babylon's Top 5 placing, though 'Please Forgive Me' had disappointed by rising no further than its Number 18 point of entry. To be fair, the original issue, way back in late 1999 before the IHT/East West pact, had spent a single week at Number 72.

'This Year's Love' entered a listing awash with 'Teenage Dirtbags' and 'Clint Eastwoods' in mid March 2001, a cautious Number 20 placing. Then like 'Please Forgive Me' it fell away meekly, falling out of the Top 75 a month later. Attempts had been made to encourage re-purchase by the hard-core faithful, the CD1 offering a 'Strings Remix' and CD2 a first-night Brixton Academy performance from three months earlier. 'Flame Turns Blue' was culled from *Lost Songs* to accompany the previously unissued 'The Lights Of London' on the first disc, while its companion offered two unknown B-sides in 'Roots Of Love' and 'Tired Of Me'.

Follow-up 'Sail Away' had proved the least successful *White Ladder*-spawned single to date at Number 26. 'Sail Away' made its début as a UK single in July 2001, following the pattern of its post-'Babylon' predecessors by entering at its highest chart position – in this case Number 26. CD1 was aimed purely at the clubbers, combining a Radio Edit with a Club Mix by Biffco and a remix by Rae & Christian Remix. The second CD entered new territory by being not merely a CD but a DVD. The A-side. if you can have such things these days, was designated as the Live At The Point Video, while further Point excepts – 30 seconds apiece – of 'This Year's Love', 'Please Forgive Me' and good old 'Wisdom' followed. Only the Biffco Radio Edit of 'Sail Away' was common to both.

David's moody monochrome cover shots were now being taken by famous society photographer Rankin (so famous he didn't need a christian name!). But DG seemed in the process of picking a spot on his cheek, so the effect was marred somewhat. . . Solace was at hand, however, as just a couple of weeks earlier *The EPs 92–94* had nudged into the album chart for a single week at Number 68. No-one could accuse Virgin of misrepresenting the product or, indeed, pushing it much at all. One ad in each major music publication seemed the extent of it.

"It's amazing how quickly you adjust," says David. "Now when a single comes out over here, I'm really disappointed when it doesn't reach the Top 20. How times have changed." But the album's success, aided by judicious TV advertising, more than made up for that. Having begun August as Number 1, it gave way to teen dream trip Atomic Kitten's 'Right Now' – ironically a revamped reissue itself– but reclaimed top spot a week later when support for the scantily-clad felines ran out of steam.

Gray's latest ascendancy of the charts was as a result of being a consistent performer in a fast-dwindling market suffering from summer
doldrums. The 35,000 weekly sales that had assured it top spot was far
inferior to its peak of 122,000 copies at Christmas 2000 – a figure
that had only been worthy of Number 13 in a chart swollen by sea-
sonal compilation offerings. Whatever, the two years and five months
that had elapsed since *White Ladder*'s appearance and it reaching
Number 1 gained it a small footnote in UK chart history. Only
Tyrannosaurus Rex's *My People Were Fair And Had Sky In Their Hair*
had surpassed that time lapse, having been swooped upon by Marc
Bolan's glam-rock following four years after release.

Maybe the secret of David Gray's appeal is that though his music
exudes a spiritual quality and he has the demeanour of a folk and
protest singer, his disdain for conventional politics and religion alike
keeps him safely in the middle of the road. Back in 1994, he'd opened
up to Colin Harper on both fronts. Asked why he didn't seem to
tackle politics in his music, except personal politics, he replied: "What
other politics *are* there? For me there aren't any others. We're all
human beings. . . I don't feel equipped – I haven't got a sufficient
enough grasp of politics and economics and all the various ludicrous
concepts that go with it to feel that I can make statements about it. I
haven't got a conviction about political technique – I just see human
things and I see things that I think are wrong.

As for religion, "I don't think you need a church to worship. I
mean, I'm not a believer but I believe in what I've got inside of me,
so that is religion in a way. Most of my songs could be interpreted as
virtually spiritual statements, which is what they are – and we're in an
age of reigning spirituality, to the detriment of everything. And I'll say
unabashedly that we need spiritual guidance – but I don't like organ-
ised religion one bit. I think it's corrupt crap, and boring as well. . ."

If the appeal of David Gray were ever encapsulated in an article
then it was Gray with added colour, published in *The Observer* on 17
December 2000. The writer was Pat Kane, formerly of Scots pop duo
Hue and Cry, and I make no apology for quoting it here verbatim
(with permission).

"By definition, a mainstream is wide, steadily flowing and deepest
in the middle. And that's exactly what you see when you stand out-

side a David Gray gig for 15 minutes or so, as they enter and then leave, profoundly satisfied at either end.

"This mainstream is made from arm-linked couples of a certain age, cargo-pant wearers and goatee sprouters, some silver surfers dragging along red-eyed student grandchildren, a wide demographic sea, without obvious shores. Security staff have turned out their pockets for weapons and bootleg recording equipment; the table shows no Stanley knives, but a profusion of mountaineering gadgets and mini-disc players.

"So it's Gray for the mainstream, the mainstream for Gray, the greyness of the mainstream. . . if you really wanted critically to dump on a gravelly-voiced singer-songwriter, playing to an mildly affluent audience yearning for even milder consolations, you could stop right there.

"But that's what rock pundits usually feel they must do to the mainstream. They are usually frightened by its size, its implacable movements, its deep undercurrents, the way that the mood of a mass of people can rip their critiques to shreds. Even more challenging when, with an artist like Gray, the energies of the mainstream are being invoked with skill, passion and authenticity.

"What happens when you make a record that talks to people right where their complex, juggled, bitter-sweet modern lives actually are? Well, this happens. A handy guy in white plimsolls, over-washed denims and a guitar comes on stage, bashfully says hello and then begins singing about 'What we gonna do when the money runs out. . . how we gonna find the eyes to see a brighter day?' Connection, big-time. That's the first rock of meaning that Gray drops in tonight's waters and it keeps rippling to the end.

"All this is not by musical chance – Gray has woven himself from some of the finer threads of the last 30 years. If you credit his biography, the singing voice, a flexible, rasping, froggy, room-filling rumble, has been conditioned by his dad playing Bob Dylan in the family car; by his youth being wasted to Van Morrison; by his wife being wooed to Tom Waits; by his tour bus being soothed by Carole King.

"The crossover twist that marks the hit records – what if Van the Man could sing to drum'n'bass? What would Dylan sound like, trancing out in Ibiza? – is faithfully reproduced here. 'Please Forgive Me' and 'Babylon' are perfectly poised between programming and performance, with Gray's lippy collaborator Clune particularly stunning on brush-drums.

"So the much-recounted tales of how *White Ladder* was conceived and recorded in the domestic bedroom, trucks outside rumbling on to the master tape, with no major deal and the money running out, make perfect sense. If Gray is trading in simplicities at the moment, it's because they're the right simplicities, tempered by experience. Find me a double-earning household in Britain where Gray's music doesn't resonate – two adults doing table-top therapy amid the Chardonnay, soggy joints and domestic bills – and I'll give you my winning Lottery ticket."

The relationship between David and East West seemed set to change to a more conventional artist-label one, as he revealed that summer in an answer to a web-question about what it was like to be his own boss. "We're about to enter into a deal here in England with Warners, which is on a completely different scale. So that truly is, um, going back on what I said! But I enjoyed the directness of being our own record company, making our own decisions." This he explained was the reason for *Lost Songs* appearing when it did.

Certainly, he seemed anxious to lose the responsibilities of a music-biz mogul, however embryonic. "I used to feel like I had to do everything myself, but all that pressure has been lifted, and it's great to work with people you believe in. The world pisses me off as much as it ever did, but I think all those hard years taught me that there are different ways of fighting. That struggle does not have to permeate your work. There are other means of protest. To do something beautiful in the face of an utterly bland, pointless music business is a form of protest," he says. "Revenge is to do something good."

This anti-commercially was reflected in his choice of reading on tour: Naomi Marks' *No Logo*, an investigation into the way designer brands like Nike (logo nickname 'swooshtika') had sewn up the fashion world. "It's a book about the corporate worlds and how the advertisement is culture itself. I'm uncomfortable with the lack of distinction between what is sacred in my eyes – like music – and multinational commerce."

He was more than happy to expand on that view. "A huge proportion of music today is just a marketing exercise. The music is inconsequential. You have no more meaning than a packet of frozen vegetables. That's always been a large part of the music industry, but the music itself used to lead the industry along. It was youth culture racing ahead and businessmen chasing it and making a mint. But now, it's business men making a mint and musicians trying to get a deal. It's a weird thing. . . the music is no longer. . . the cart is leading the horse."

His heroes in bucking the corporate rock trend were Radiohead, "because they're not going to have Heineken or Guinness written across the tent – it's about playing music not some shit producer nobody needs." Conversely, Moby was "the biggest twat of all because he still talks the talk as if he has some integrity. 'I'll get on every advert known to man, and then I'll talk about the environment.' Shut up!"

It's a viewpoint he'd held throughout his career. Back in 1994, he'd sounded off in familiar style to Colin Harper. "I get more outraged by billboard adverts than I do about music business reunions. Nothing surprises me about what the music business will do for a cheap trick. It's a sad fucking industry. It works the same as any industry and that's why it's sad – because it's dealing with something precious. You can see why forces prevail – it's about money basically. Unfortunately there's quite a fragile human process right at the root of it, which is making music, which can be easily destroyed by its rather heavy-handed techniques."

It was too early to say how the follow-up to *White Ladder* would sound, or indeed if it would present a deliberately non-commercial face to the world. "I'm looking for a surprise. I don't have an idea really. There's lots of concepts that I want to sort of experiment with as far as how the process goes of making a song. . . or whatever. So, I really don't have a clue. I'm hoping it surprises me. As for moving further into the world of dance music, "I don't think that's realistic." But then realism had played little part in David Gray's rise to fame. In sporting terms, he had 'done a Wimbledon' – risen from the non-League doldrums to the Premier League of rock music. He'd achieved this on a decidedly non-League budget, and by making the most of the resources available to him. The problem he now faced was similar to that of his beloved Manchester United – how to make sure his success was sustained.

In interviews, he'd been careful to distance himself from the club's many celebrity fans – the so-called 'prawn sandwich brigade'. "I was brought up in Manchester and I used to go to their games when I was little. They've become phenomenally successful in the Nineties but I supported them when they were crap. I'm a big football fan and they're the biggest and best team."

From Sale to Babylon via Solva, Stoke Newington and Old Trafford. . . what a long strange trip it had been. And there was more to come.

Back in 1994, Gray had outlined his modest ambitions to Colin Harper thus: "My goals, what I dream about, aren't really in keeping with the reality of being a megastar in the music business – that doesn't appeal to me at all. The idea of playing big gigs does, and making definitive records does – you know, I haven't reached my peak yet. I'm learning all the time more about what I do, and I always will be as long as I keep doing it."

When in 2001 he was asked how he described his music, David first deflected the question by saying he'd "leave that to the people." But he them seemed compelled to continue. "I'll bump into someone on holiday and they'll say, 'Well, what's your music like?' and I'll say 'Ah, you know, Bob Dylan, Van Morrison, but a bit more contemporary. . . with beat.' That's my condensing it to a sentence. I wouldn't like it to be described to me like that, but it's hard to find the right words.

"I know that I've only just started learning how it all fits together. I'm just at the beginning of my creative mountain, and I think most of these people are well up at the peak." Only time would tell how high David Gray's own creative mountain would rise.

CHAPTER 11

The Other Side

The year of 2001 ended with a fifth single from *White Ladder* – and given the airplay it had already received, it was little surprise that the familiar 'Say Hello Wave Goodbye' should be accorded belated release in its own right. It charted three days before Christmas at Number 26, slipping to 29 a week later and falling to 40 on January 7, 2002 – a profile remarkably similar to its predecessor, 'Sail Away'.

The coming year would see family matters take precedence in Gray's life – and the singer knew full well things would never be the same after the appearance of his first-born, Ivy. "The birth didn't go well," he confided to *Q* magazine, "and we were in hospital for a long time. When we got home Olivia was worn out, so there was no way I could go back to work. And the baby took over – surprise, surprise!"

Ivy's arrival would mean that David would no longer be the road warrior of old, where "all you've got is these blokes who fart and throw joints at you." Henceforth, pared-down tour itineraries would lean heavily on high volume/prestige venues such as London's Earl's Court or Madison Square Garden in New York. Nevertheless, Gray hoped the 'birth' of a new album would give him the chance to visit hitherto un-gigged places where *White Ladder* had done well: Australia, New Zealand, Italy and Spain were favourites.

Ah, yes – a new album. . .

Four years on from *White Ladder*, David Gray unveiled *A New Day At Midnight*, trailed by his website as "12 world-class songs from a small room in south London." (A bigger studio had been tried, but had not yielded successful results.) It emerged in October 2002, finding itself, intentionally or otherwise, overshadowed by the customary slew of hits collections from a music business desperate to wring every drop of profit it could out of past glories – or back catalogue, as the jargon has it.

Not that any were likely to rival the performance of *White Ladder*. At the time of its successor's release, David's 'greatest hit' had clocked up more than 100 weeks in the UK Top 40 and been certified seven times platinum with sales of over 2.2 million. A similar number of records had been shifted in the States, while in Ireland, the country where it had all begun, *White Ladder* had written itself into history by virtue of a staggering 175 weeks on the chart. Not only that, it was now the biggest selling non-compilation album of all time there.

Most performers, no matter how self-confident, would be overwhelmed by the need to follow up such success. But Gray, having bought himself valuable thinking time with 'Lost Songs', had made the most of it, creating around 20 new numbers in *White Ladder* vein, only to shelve them all after his father's death in February 2001. A week later, he'd penned 'Last Boat To America', while 'Freedom' was the first he'd commit to tape when re-entering the studio. His quality control threshold then went up several notches. "I balanced (those two songs) against the others," he reflected, "and that told me all I needed to know (about their relative merits)."

The sessions took place in David's six by three metre Clapham studio, beginning in spring 2001 but mainly in the six months leading up to August 2002. As has been hinted, his tried and tested team of Clune and Lestyn Polson were left holding the master tapes as Gray held the baby, the pair sending their 'boss' track mixes for him to comment on and feed back telephonically. He had kept on writing right up until the mixing process began, standout and first single 'The

Other Side' having been recorded a matter of a few days before they shut the studio door. Indeed, 'The Other Side' was to win both his UK and US record companies' vote for first single, David having seemingly ceded the power of choice when renegotiating his contract. Released in early December, the song was paired with two album out-takes in 'Decipher' and 'Lorelei'. Spookily, it became the third single in succession to peak at Number 26...

But on to the album. Opener 'Dead In The Water' was, according to one review, "a fine example of Gray's ability to fuse a positive outlook with melancholy". Certainly, its writer conceded the song's lyrics had "a bit more of an edge to them." He saw this album as a whole, and this song in particular, as harking back to "the old-style 'Birds Without Wings'/'Let The Truth Sting' approach", something that distinguished it from *White Ladder*, with its "lightness of touch". After 'Caroline', a song about a "steel-eyed dinosaur" that appropriately featured steel guitar from top sessioneer BJ Cole, and the low-key, percussion-laced 'Long Distance Call' came the previously-highlighted 'Freedom', which distinguished itself by being a seven minute-long, almost politically charged ballad ('a world that's lost its meaning/ain't no kind of freedom') with a Hovis ad-style brass section.

The more upbeat 'Real Love' was familiar from Gray's US *White Ladder* tour, as was 'Last Boat To America' and the Train-esque future single 'Be Mine'. (Other recent live staples 'All The Love' and 'Longest Time' were, however, conspicuously absent.) 'December' boasted both dark lyrics – 'Killers underneath our skins' – and a suitably unsettling vocal over tremulous piano.

Unusual instruments had played a part in the recording process: 'Real Love' had featured a dulcimer, while the loping, off-beat 'Kangaroo' was embellished with a melodica (a mouth-powered keyboard) popular with reggae musicians. An attempt to use steel drums took up a day and came to nothing, however. 'Knowhere' was credited to David and bassist Rob Malone while 'Easy Way To Cry' was singled out in *Q* magazine's four-star review as "feeble".

The instrumental expertise of Tim Bradshaw was evident on seven songs, his contributions ranging from piano, electric guitar and lap steel to backwards synth and drone keys. Clune (or McClune, as he was credited) co-wrote 'Real Love' and 'Be Mine', while playing all otherwise unattributed instruments along with David. The album ended with the previously mentioned 'The Other Side', a raw, emotional song clearly inspired by the death of David's father. "I have no belief that I will meet (him) again," he said, "but in this song I'm calling out and wishing I could." The underlying theme of *A New Day At Midnight* was loss, but also hope. "As the title expresses, there's a vividness to life even at the bleakest, darkest moments."

It was certainly a bright moment when, on November 9, *A New Day At Midnight* beat off considerable competition to debut at Number One in the UK album chart. With *Pop Idol's* Gareth Gates, Nirvana and Manic Street Preachers (both the last named hits collections) all released in the same week, and a new Foo Fighters album only just arrived at the top this had been by no means a foregone conclusion.

Teen heart-throbs Blue and another compilation from U2 conspired to limit David to a single week at the top, but it took only three weeks to notch up 300,000 (platinum) sales. That had been tripled by the time it fell out of the Top 20 in January 2003, by which time *White Ladder* had re-entered the Top 40 in its 139th chart week, undoubtedly buoyed by David's pre-Christmas UK tour. But could there be many British households that didn't have a copy already?

The radio-friendly 'Be Mine' – acclaimed by *Q's* reviewer as "probably the song of David Gray's life" – was issued as a second single. It was sensibly cut down to two verses from the original three, but inexplicably missed the logical Valentine's Day release date by almost two months. It therefore failed to do a 'This Year's Love', peaking at Number 21, but rewarded purchasers with bonus tracks 'Lover Boy' (a new song) and a live version of *Lost Songs* favourite 'Falling Down The Mountainside'.

The day after Valentine's Day had seen David playing the Bill Graham Civic Auditorium in San Francisco, the penultimate date of a three-week North American tour. Instead of employing an opening act, David and his four-piece band played two sets; the first opened on an *avant garde* note with a version of Orbital's instrumental 'Lush 3-1'. Kicking off the vocal numbers with 'Dead In The Water', followed without a pause by the title track from *White Ladder*, David spent the first set switching between the two albums at will. Oldies 'Everytime' and 'Late Night Radio' were thrown in for long-time fans before he chose the end of the first set to get 'Babylon' out of the way. The arrangement was changed just enough to catch the ear, while retaining the familiar frisson.

The second set opened with Gray serenading the audience from in front of a closed stage curtain, following an acoustic 'This Year's Love', with a bass-accompanied version of Van Morrison's classic 'And It Stoned Me'. Comparisons confronted, the mini set concluded with 'Coming Down', a song from second album *Flesh* he explained he'd written with Olivia in mind the last time he was in San Francisco without her. The song was concluded despite a broken string (evoking a good-natured curse of "bollocks!") before the room erupted in approval. The curtains then opened to reveal a shirtless Clune, who proceeded to power his fellow musicians through 'Freedom', 'Say Hello Wave Goodbye' and a closing, triumphant 'Please Forgive Me'. As ever, no apologies were necessary.

March saw David visit nine European countries in the space of 16 breakneck dates. And though he finally got to Australia and New Zealand in May as hoped, proposed shows in Hong Kong and Singapore *en route* had to be cancelled due to the spread of the deadly SARS virus. "It was David's strong desire to fulfil the dates despite the very difficult situation, if at all prudent to do so," said his management – but with The Rolling Stones cancelling their first ever dates behind the Bamboo Curtain it was clearly prudent for DG to reschedule the two shows.

While he was away, David became the recipient of a second Ivor Novello Award, the first having been for 'Babylon' back in 2001. As then, the category was Best Song Musically and Lyrically this time for 'The Other Side'; Travis and U2 were among those he beat to the prestigious songwriting award. A Brit nomination earlier in the year had seen him compete with Badly Drawn Boy, The Streets, Craig David and eventual winner Robbie Williams for the title of Best Male Solo Artist, but there was little doubt the 'Ivor' meant more to this proud songwriter.

The summer of 2003 was to start with a single Irish date in Killarney before a Glastonbury appearance. Then, after three weeks with the family, he packed his flight cases once more for another Stateside jaunt in the company of Turin Brakes and familiar touring partner Nelly Furtado. Kicking off in San Diego, the string of dates ended three weeks later in Hartford, Connecticut, in mid-July. August brought an Edinburgh appearance as part of the T on the Fringe festival before the demands of V2003 in Staffordshire and Chelmsford, where he shared billing with the Red Hot Chili Peppers.

But the most notable gig of David Gray's festival summer was surely the free concert he gave with guests Morcheeba in the very centre of London on the last day of August. The dual intention was to mark the re-opening of a redeveloped Trafalgar Square with its newly pedestrianised (and allegedly pigeonless) north side and to celebrate culture in the capital, the invitation having been extended by London mayor and DG fan Ken Livingstone. Not that everyone agreed with the newt lover's choice: former *New Musical Express* hack Danny Baker, now Radio London's breakfast host, sounded off loudly, while fellow DJ John Gaunt bemoaned the fact that Ken had chosen "someone whose entire career rests on the fact he can't get his rocks off".

That could certainly not be said of the 12,000 ticketholders who revelled until midnight as David's lightshow lit up the National Gallery at his rear as it had never been illuminated before. "The opportunity of playing a free concert in central London doesn't present itself very often," the 'Welsh' singer told the *Guardian* of a show unrivalled since 2001's South African Freedom Day gig in 2001, while Lee Harley from Medway, Kent, was simply happy to celebrate his eighth wedding anniversary with his nearest and dearest. "David Gray is a big thing for us, because his song 'This Year's Love' is our song," he explained.

And maybe that was Gray's secret — the ability to reduce London's most famous square to the size of the Harleys' front room. Had he a white ladder to hand, Horatio Nelson himself might have hopped down to join in the festivities. Only the 88,000 disappointed ticket applicants could have had cause for complaint. But there'd be other times... because David Gray, like the statuesque Lord staring down at him, looked unlikely to go the way of the pigeons any time soon.

UK Discography

Singles

Birds Without Wings/L's Song/The Light
Hut Records HUTCD 23; November 1992

Shine/Brick Walls/The Rice
Hut Records HUTCD 27; March 1993

Wisdom/Lovers/4AM
Hut Records – HUTCD 32; July 4, 1993

This Year's Love/Nightblindness/Over My Head
IHT Records IHTCDS001; 1998

Babylon/Lead Me Upstairs (Live)/New Horizons (Live)
IHT Records IHTCDS002; 1998

Please Forgive Me/Paul Hartnoll remix
IHT Records IHTCDS003; 1999

Babylon (Re-release)/Over My Head/Tell Me More Lies
East West Records EW215; June 2000

Please Forgive Me (Re-release)/Please Forgive Me (Hartnoll
remix)/Babylon (Live from The Point, Dublin, 22 December 1999)
East West Records EW219; October 2000

This Year's Love (Re-release)/Flame Turns Blue/The Lights of
London (Strings Remix)
East West Records EW228CD1; March 2001

This Year's Love (Re-release) (Live At The Brixton Academy
16/12/00)/ Roots Of Love/Tired of Me (Live in London)
East West Records EW228CD2; March 2001

Sail Away (Biffco Radio Edit)/Sail Away (Biffco Club Mix)/Sail
Away (Rae & Christian Remix)
East West Records – EW234CD; July 2001

Sail Away (Live At The Point Video)/Sail Away (Biffco Radio
Edit)/This Year's Love (Live At The Point Excerpt)/Please Forgive
Me (Live At The Point Excerpt)/ Wisdom (Live At The Point
Excerpt)
East West Records – EW234DVD; July 2001

Say Hello Wave Goodbye/Say Hello Wave Goodbye (Edit)
East West Records - EW244CD; December 17, 2001

The Other Side/Decipher/Lorelei
East West Records - EW259CD; December 9, 2002

Be Mine/Be Mine (Radio Remix)/ Loverboy/Falling Down The
Mountainside (Live)
East West Records - EW264CD; April 7, 2003

Albums
A Century Ends
Shine/A Century Ends/Debauchery/Let The Truth
Sting/Gathering Dust/Wisdom/ Lead Me Upstairs/Living
Room/Birds Without Wings/It's All Over
Hut Records CDHUT 9; June 1993

Flesh
What Are You?/The Light/Coming Down/Falling Free/Made Up
My Mind/Mystery Of Love/Lullaby/New Horizons/Love's Old

Song/Flesh
Hut Records CDHUT 17; September 1994

Sell, Sell, Sell
Faster, Sooner, Now/Late Night Radio/Sell, Sell, Sell/Hold On To
Nothing/ Everytime/Magdelena/Smile/Only The Lonely/What
Am I Doing Wrong?/Gutters Full Of Rain/Forever Is Tomorrow Is
Today/Folk Song
EMI Records 7243 8 37357 2 3; 1996

White Ladder
Can't Get Through (hidden track)/Please Forgive Me/Babylon/My
Oh My/We're Not Right/Silver Lining/White Ladder/This Year's
Love/Sail Away/Say Hello Wave Goodbye
Originally released on IHT Records (November 1998), then re-
released as East West Records 857382983 2; May 2000 (East West
version includes Nightblindness as bonus track.)

Lost Songs 95–98
Flame Turns Blue/Twilight/Hold On/As I'm Leaving/If Your Love
Is Real/Tidal Wave/Falling Down The Mountainside/January
Moon/Red Moon/Clean Pair Of Eyes
East West 8573-86953-2; February 2001 (Originally released in
Ireland on IHT in June 2000)

The EPs 92–94
Birds Without Wings/L's Song/The Light/Shine/Brick Walls/The
Rice/Wisdom/
Lovers/4AM/Coming Down/Shine – The Video/Wisdom – The Video
Hut Records CD HUT 67; July 2001

A New Day At Midnight
Dead In The Water, Caroline, Long Distance Call, Freedom,
Kangaroo, Last Boat To America, Real Love, Knowhere, December,
Be Mine, Easy Way To Cry, The Other Side
East West Records 5050466-1078-2-4; October 2002

Video & DVD
David Gray Live
(Warner Music 8573859982)
1. Sail Away 2. White Ladder 3. Late Night Radio 4. Faster, Sooner, Now 5. Lead Me Upstairs 6. Babylon 7. The Light 8. We're Not Right 9. Flame Turns Blue 10. This Years Love 11. Coming Down 12. Shine 13. A Century Ends 14. My Oh My 15. Wisdom 16. Silver Lining 17. Please Forgive Me
The video includes an interview.
The DVD includes a 52-minute documentary, Up To A Point.

Promos
Flesh Promo
Made Up My Mind/What Are You?/Falling Free/Coming Down
Hut Records CDHUTP 17

Flame Turns Blue
Released: 2000 (Ireland only)
IHT Records
One track promo to promote the Lost Songs album release.

Babylon (Flightcrank remix)
East West Records
Released only on vinyl in a printed silver sleeve for DJ use. The record's label doesn't mention David Gray's name.

Babylon (UK Promo)
Released: 2000
East West Records SAM00301
Two different radio versions of the song

Please Forgive Me (UK Promo)
IHT Records IHTCDSP003
A UK promo for the single release
B-Sides: Radio edit Remix Radio Edit

Please Forgive Me (UK DJ Promo)
Released 1999
IHT Records IHTCDS003
Orbital remix

Compilations featuring David Gray songs
Stuck on Caroline (A Caroline sampler CD)
Caroline VVSAM 22; 1993
Features A Century Ends, L's Song plus Shine by Walt Mink.

Signed, Sealed, Delivered
Virgin – VVSAM 22; 1994
Features What Are You?

The Sound Of Hut
Hut Recordings (Cassette only); 1994
Features Lovers

Liss Ard
Garden's Voice; 1997
Features Falling Free, Birds Without Wings
Released after Gray played at the Liss Ard '97 festival.

This Year's Love
Soundtrack
V2 Records VVR1006362
Features This Year's Love, Monday Morning

Silver & Gold
HotPress Ireland Ltd; December 1999
Features Tell Me More Lies
Given Away with *Hot Press* Annual 1999

Enter Interactive Volume 1 (Video)
Pure Communications, Ireland; December 1999
Features Babylon (solo, acoustic), Interview snippets

Best Tracks From The Best Albums of 2000
Q Magazine; January 2001
Features We're Not Right

Now 47
EMI Records; November, 2000
Features Babylon

KBCO – Studio C Volume 12
KBCO 97.3FM; December 2000
Features Babylon (live)
A locally released album in Boulder, Colorado by radio station
KBCO to benefit a local AIDS charity. The version of 'Babylon'
included on this CD was recorded in the studio during an interview
with David.

Various Artists
Party In the Park
2CD (Universal Music TV 585 000 2)
Features Babylon plus video of performance